Pursue Your Freedom and Happiness

Break Free From Dysfunctional Organizations.

Invest in Yourself.

Build Long-Term Success.

Chris Banescu

Creative illumination Publishing
Santa Clarita, CA

Creative Illumination Publishing
Santa Clarita, CA

Copyright © 2020 by Chris Banescu

ISBN 978-1-7357686-0-1

This book is dedicated to my mom, Margaret,
who taught me the value of courage and freedom.

She defied tyranny and escaped communism
to give me freedom.
She sacrificed and endured much so I could be free.
She showed me that love is an action, not just a feeling.

Chris Bane

Contents

Contents

CHAPTER 1

Your Personal Declaration of Independence

*We hold these truths to be self-evident, that all men are
created equal, that they are endowed by their Creator
with certain unalienable Rights, that among these are
Life, Liberty and the pursuit of Happiness.*

—Declaration of Independence, July 4, 1776

The human soul yearns for freedom. The human heart was
created to desire happiness and joy. The human mind was
designed to seek the truth. The human will is fueled by hope.
These are universal truths that have been virtually ignored by
most companies and organizations. Instead, management
treats human beings as interchangeable parts of a machine or
disposable components of a system, to exploit and carelessly
toss aside on a whim. This is a human catastrophe of monu-
mental proportions. This is unacceptable. This is wrong.

Many of us approach our jobs with a sense of resignation
and even dread. We work for companies and institutions that
do not appreciate us or treat us fairly, but still expect us to
sacrifice our time and health for their sole benefit without
proportional or just compensation. We report to unqualified,
unethical, or egotistical managers who don't respect us, don't
care for us, and rarely bother to recognize our worth and reward our contributions adequately; but still demand our

unconditional obedience and unquestioning loyalty.

Many of us have invested years or even decades of hard work and loyal service to support and grow businesses and organizations, only to see it arbitrarily taken away from us without warning and due process; often due to the manipulation, selfishness, ineptitude, or greed of less capable, less experienced, and less deserving individuals.

Wrong People Are In Charge

This book bears witness that what's happened and is now happening to us is a travesty. Too many companies, organizations, and institutions mismanage employees and squander their resources. The wrong leaders are in charge. The wrong people are being promoted and given more responsibility. Incompetent, unprincipled, or abusive employees seem to continually rise to the top. Their behavior and management style contradict the actual principles and ideals that managers and leaders should follow and practice. They demotivate employees, crush their spirit, and undermine their creativity and productivity. They alienate customers and negatively affect profitability. They destroy the company from the inside. Yet, these dysfunctional individuals thrive and prosper, while we suffer and struggle even though we continue to give our best.

My heartfelt message goes out to all those who at one time or another felt frustrated, alone, unappreciated, ignored, marginalized, insulted, belittled, abused, and discarded by management and superiors at various organizational levels. This call goes out to the millions of individuals who have, at one time or another, encountered any one of the many examples and scenarios included in this book and walked away thinking that maybe they are to blame; that something is wrong with their expectations; that they're too idealistic; that they're being unreasonable; that it's their fault; that they may be crazy.

It's Not You, It's Them!

I'm here to tell you that it's not your fault. You are not unreasonable. You are not too idealistic. You are not crazy. It's not you, it's them! You have intuitively sensed that something is not right with your supervisors, managers, executives, or bosses. You have correctly observed that something's definitely wrong with the company, organization, or institution where you work. You have wisely noticed that the way "things are done around here" is not ethical, logical, productive, fair, or just. You are seeing things as they really are. You're rightly perceiving that something is terribly amiss in your workplace. It looks like the organization is heading in the wrong direction. It appears that the worst people have all the power and influence. Most days it seems like the inmates are running the asylum. Guess what? You're right!

The long journey that brought me here is one of many trials, tribulations, suffering, and personal struggles. But it's also a journey filled with great experiences, discoveries, and wonderful moments of happiness, peace, joy, success, and liberation. I have traveled the same road as you and experienced first-hand many of the same problems, abuses, troubles, and dilemmas you have faced or are now facing. I've been where you are and experienced what you're going through. I understand the confusion, the alienation, the sense of betrayal, the fear, the feeling of hopelessness, the pain, the despair, and the many disappointments. I sympathize with your situation and your righteous indignation.

Help is Here

This book is written to help you. It will remind you of important truths, universal principles, and timeless wisdom you can draw from and apply in your own life. It can be referenced in both personal and professional settings, for personal growth and enlightenment. The book can be used as a survival guide to help you cope with the storms of dysfunction, incompetence, and unethical behavior raging in many organizations. You can also use it to evaluate your current workplace and its management, to either appreciate them, if indeed they are worthy of such praise, or protect yourself and seek better opportunities elsewhere, if you discover that they are hazardous to your career or well-being. Finally, if you work for an average or mediocre company that needs help, there are opportunities for improvement, and you have managers who are willing to listen and change—and won't fire you for speaking up—you can reference this book for guidance on what to do.

And if you have already achieved a reasonable level of freedom and independence—either by owning your own business or reaching the higher level of executive leadership in a great organization—this book can reinforce key principles to remember and continually practice. These concepts will help you maintain a healthy, productive, and thriving culture in your organization. The book will also warn you of mistakes and dangers to avoid.

No More Pearls Before Swine

If you already know or now realize (while reading this book) that you work for a dysfunctional, highly dysfunctional, or toxic organization, you need to plan your escape and leave. It's time to say no more! It's time to reject the lies you've been told and the insults and abuses you've had to accept and endure. Stop giving your best to those who don't appreciate it and don't deserve it. Stop giving your pearls, your unique talents, to swine. Use those pearls to escape the dysfunction you've had to tolerate. Invest those pearls in your own future and your own success. Use those pearls to buy back your freedom. Invest your pearls to regain your dignity and peace of mind and soul. Use those pearls to live a better life and thrive.

I have written this book as a beacon of hope to support, reassure, and guide you on your own journey towards a more meaningful and fulfilled life. I hope it will open your heart and mind to see reality around you more clearly and begin the process of liberation both on a spiritual and material level; often one cannot exist without the other. I want to inspire and motivate you to pursue your God-given freedom and seek genuine happiness.

It's time to issue your own personal Declaration of Independence, fight back to regain your freedom, and begin the journey to recapture your *unalienable rights:* your *life, liberty and the pursuit of happiness.*

You have wasted too much time just existing, struggling, and surviving, it's time to start living!

CHAPTER 2

This is a Revolution, Not Just a Book

When you want to help people, you tell them the truth.
When you want to help yourself,
you tell them what they want to hear.

—Thomas Sowell

I want to start a Revolution, not just sell you a book. It's a creative revolution, a peaceful revolution, with no violence, no mayhem, and no killing. A revolution to free you from the abuses you endure at work and the lies you're constantly told. A revolution to liberate yourself from the fears and falsehoods that undermine your self-confidence and success. A revolution to bring truth, meaning, hope, and joy into your life, all of your life; at work and at home. A revolution to let you taste liberty and happiness as they should be experienced. A revolution that ultimately starves dysfunctional and toxic organizations of their resources, and leads to their demise. A revolution that rewards healthy organizations, great businesses, and vibrant companies by allowing them to hire more employees who escape from toxic workplaces. A revolution that helps decent organizations and good people succeed and thrive.

This book is much more than just another self-help, seek

success, motivational book. There are plenty of those books out there. This book should be read first, before you read the others! Why? Because this book deals with the circumstances of your workplace situation, career, and life as they are today. It provides useful knowledge and practical advice to use for your benefit. It presents raw truths you need to know to see things clearly, understand them accurately, and act appropriately. It gives you the means to free yourself from those things that negatively impact your health, your life, and your future.

The book exposes the warning signs of poorly-managed organizations and contrasts them with the characteristics of healthy companies. It teaches you how to take immediate action to help yourself in a realistic and meaningful manner. It provides the missing piece that other self-help books often lack. It offers practical advice on how to identify, evaluate, explain, and effectively deal with the problems you presently face. It recommends tactics to handle the incompetent, unethical, and downright nasty individuals you encounter at work. It suggests ways to protect yourself and minimize the damage inflicted on you. It teaches you how to diminish the power and control that malicious bosses or unscrupulous co-workers exert over you.

My primary goals are to: (1) tell you the truth, (2) sharpen your understanding, (3) inspire you to face reality and take action, (4) motivate you to find better opportunities so you can thrive and be successful, and (5) prepare you for the long-term journey to pursue your freedom and happiness.

My secondary goals are to: (1) boost your self-confidence and resolve, (2) help you fix problems with your current work situation, if it's possible, and (3) recommend ways to bring about positive changes to your current organization, if it's feasible.

The Book I Wish I Had Read

This is the book I wish I had read when I was younger. This is the book I wish I had read when I:

- worked in my first job,
- encountered my first incompetent boss,
- was repeatedly lied to by deceitful managers,
- was manipulated by treacherous superiors,
- was screamed at by an abusive executive,
- was mislead by scheming co-workers,
- was arbitrarily passed over for promotion,
- was belittled for standing up for myself,
- was admonished for speaking the truth,
- was ostracized for acting ethically,
- was reprimanded for trying to improve things,
- was punished for doing what's right, or
- was laid off for questioning unethical and dysfunctional executives.

This book would have saved me—and now will hopefully save you—a lot of wasted time, effort, and energy; save you from unnecessary heartaches and suffering; and help you seek a better and healthier work environment and culture somewhere else. I would have started to *dig my tunnel* a lot sooner to escape the unhealthy companies and organizations that took advantage of me and abused me. Those dysfunctional workplaces used my specific abilities, innocence, truthfulness, and work ethic against me. Unprincipled managers and unethical executives exploited my skills and efforts to reward themselves and their undeserving lackeys.

Dig Your Tunnel

I wish to persuade you to escape dysfunctional and toxic organizations, because the risks of staying far outweigh the risks of leaving. I want to show you how to "dig your tunnel" and not lose your current job too soon, before you're ready to quit. Be prudent and smart about when and how you get away. This is where this book will come in handy. Prepare and plan carefully, undetected by your current untrustworthy boss or fellow co-workers. If they find out, some will either persuade you to stay, attempt to prevent you from leaving, make your life even more miserable, or get you fired before you're ready to leave.

That's why I call this process "digging your tunnel." I use the imagery of an innocent prisoner who is wrongly convicted and locked up in prison. He is unable to find justice through normal channels. He cannot prove his innocence through due process. The system is too corrupt. Having exhausted all appeals and unwilling to spend the rest of his life behind bars for a crime he did not commit, he takes matters into his own hands. He secretly plans his escape and begins to dig his tunnel. Finally, after years of toil and daily effort, in secret, he completes the tunnel and gets away. He flees and goes on to live life on his own terms as a free man, in a different part of the world where individual liberty, truth, and due process matter; and corruption has not compromised the justice system.

Nothing in Life Worth Having Comes Easy

I'm going to tell you the truth. Tell it to you like it is. I won't soften it or sugarcoat it, like some self-help gurus do. Just wishing it to happen, won't make it happen. Just thinking positive thoughts won't attract success. Positive affirmations (as important as they are) alone won't provide meaning, bring you wealth, or solve your problems. A positive mindset is critical, but it must be grounded in reality and accompanied by wise planning, hard work, and consistent progress in the right direction. To be effective, optimism needs to be supplemented by determination, proper focus, and purposeful action. That's how you earn your freedom and happiness. That's how most successful individuals have earned theirs.

Improving yourself is only half the equation; most other self-improvement books cover this well. You should also truthfully discern and evaluate the reality around you in order to avoid mistakes, spot deceivers and minimize their influence over you, defend yourself, take corrective action immediately, and make the right decisions for your future. This is where this book will help you with practical guidance and worthwhile advice you can apply right away.

Digging your tunnel and earning your freedom will take time and demand sacrifices, effort, commitment, and discipline on your part. Nothing in life worth having comes easy. There are no shortcuts to success, in any worthy endeavor. Be patient and resolute. Stay the course and persevere. Never give up. The results you will achieve, the self-confidence you will gain, the happiness you will experience, and the freedom you will regain, are absolutely worth it.

It's better to stand on your own two feet with honor and integrity, be in control of your own destiny, earn your living doing something worthwhile, work alongside decent and honest people, and be appreciated for your efforts, than be dependent on an organization that doesn't care about you or remain subservient to a boss who regularly lies to you, manipulates you, or abuses you—especially when both can and will get rid of you at any time for any reason.

How To Use This Book
People need to be reminded more often than
they need to be instructed.
—Samuel Johnson

Use and apply this book in whole or in part, in the manner that's most useful to you. Read it in full and then re-read only those chapters that look interesting or are relevant to your current situation. Each chapter has a specific theme and can be read independently of the others.

I highly recommend reading the entire book all the way through at least once. You will have a better understanding of all the practical real-world advice and key principles covered. They should help you gain valuable insights on how to protect yourself and pursue your freedom.

Only the first eight chapters should be read in order. They establish a solid foundation for the remaining chapters. Chapters one through eight provide the necessary principles, definitions, and support to guide you in subsequent pages. The rest of the chapters can be read in any order you wish.

Re-read and Reference When Needed
To re-read a book is to read a different book.
The reader is different. The meaning is different.
—Johnny Rich

You should hold on to this book, because certain sections may become relevant in the future. The content will remain the same, but you'll be different. As your career progresses and work situations change, or your own business grows, new issues or conflicts may appear that you didn't previously encounter. Re-read the book when that happens for additional guidance and insights to apply to those new circumstances. Chapters that you originally read for educational value can suddenly become more meaningful and personal. Previously, those chapters seemed to present only information and broad expertise. Now, they offer you a lifeline to truth and sanity, or a much needed reality check on what's really going on at work, in your own business, or in your personal life. The chapters haven't changed, but you have.

Think of this book also as a toolbox of knowledge and wisdom. Use it to apply the right tool(s) for a specific situation. Reference it when evaluating new opportunities. Review it when considering a promotion or a career change. Reach for it when you encounter new problems or dilemmas. Re-read it for suggestions and recommendations on how to spot and address new dysfunctions or conflicts. Read it when you need some common sense.

Reach for this book every time you feel yourself drifting away from your goals and need a solid dose of reality. Use it to remind yourself of important and timeless principles required for success and financial prosperity. Rely on it for reassurance, encouragement, inspiration, and motivation to persevere and continue on your journey in pursuit of freedom and happiness.

CHAPTER 3

Gain Clarity on Freedom, Happiness, and Success

*Our greatest happiness does not depend on the condition
of life in which chance has placed us, but is always the
result of a good conscience, good health, occupation,
and freedom in all just pursuits.*
—Thomas Jefferson

Words like *freedom*, *happiness*, and *success* mean many different things to different people. As the culture around us has become increasingly dysfunctional and superficial, the very definitions and usage of words have changed. I'm a firm believer in clarity and the power of words to accurately describe reality and express truth. Before proceeding, I dedicate a chapter to properly define *freedom*, *happiness*, and *success*.

Freedom
*Every human has four endowments – self-awareness,
conscience, independent will and creative imagination.
These give us the ultimate human freedom...The power
to choose, to respond, to change.*
—Stephen Covey

The *freedom* this book talks about is multi-dimensional. It means your individual freedom to voluntarily choose how you want to live your life and follow your own path. It encompasses your ability to change, improve, and pursue what you consider important, valuable, and meaningful. It entails your personal freedom as an individual living in a free and democratic society governed by the rule of law. It also includes your financial, mental, and economic freedom. All these elements should co-exist for us to truly experience, enjoy, and preserve our freedom.

First and foremost, freedom and truth are inseparably linked. Without truth, real freedom begins to disappear. Like freedom, we must pursue truth in all things and at all times, otherwise we get ourselves into trouble and expose ourselves to dangerous people and situations. When truth is ignored, distorted, or silenced, freedom disappears and disasters ultimately follow. This is universally true not only in our personal lives, but also in the companies and organizations where we work and in society at large. (Please see Chapter 8, "Live in Reality, Seek the Truth" that covers this topic in greater detail.)

Second, always use your freedom constructively and wisely. Rely on it to pursue excellence in all things. Use it to improve yourself, seek understanding, enhance your knowledge, increase your wisdom, and implement positive changes in your life. Apply it to become a good person and a great leader that others respect, trust, and willingly follow. Rely on it to achieve personal freedom from bad habits, negative thoughts, self-defeating behavior, unreasonable fears, and harmful character traits. Employ it to end your financial reliance and psychological dependence on wrong people and toxic organizations. Use it to follow better opportunities and achieve financial stability and prosperity. Rely on it to pursue what you're passionate about and have an aptitude for—and to focus on what's meaningful and valuable to you.

Third, with freedom comes great responsibility and accountability. The exercise of our freedom cannot come at the expense of others. We need to respect their freedom. We have to act responsibly and sensibly. Our freedom cannot injure others, limit their fundamental personal freedom, negatively affect their economic freedom, or destroy their property. We have to be accountable to ourselves and those around us. The pursuit and enjoyment of our freedom cannot affect the right and ability of others to pursue theirs. Same principle ought to apply in all organizational settings, but it rarely does.

Finally, remain vigilant. Freedom can be misused to your own detriment. Just because something is permissible or legal in a free society, it doesn't mean you should indulge in it. When you abuse your freedom it will destroy you and your future. Don't do anything stupid—take illegal drugs, abuse alcohol, gamble compulsively, become addicted to pornography, cheat on your spouse—that harms your body, damages your mind, or corrupts your soul. Exercising that kind of "freedom" will always enslave you and lead to your eventual destruction. It can also lead to loss of financial freedom (lawsuits, divorce, bankruptcy), loss of physical freedom (jail time), loss of mental freedom (neurosis, psychosis, insanity), or loss of life (heart attack, stroke, drug overdose, suicide).

Happiness

Throw yourself into some work you believe in with all your heart, live for it, die for it, and you will find the happiness that you had thought could never be yours.

—Dale Carnegie

Like freedom, *happiness* has many different connotations. You may have already determined what happiness means to you. If you're happy with that choice, then keep on using it. If you haven't thought about this previously, I hope you'll be persuaded to adopt the definition of happiness I prefer to use.

The kind of happiness I pursue and talk about in this book, is more than an emotion or a feeling of contentment or pleasure. The happiness I'm referring to comes closest to what's typically called *joy*. It's difficult to fully define joy since each of us may experience it in unique and special ways.

For myself, when I experience true happiness (joy) it encompasses not only feelings of contentment and pleasure, but it includes other qualities. I sense inner peace, combined with exuberance. The effects of joy are transformative. My soul is filled with optimism. My heart feels hope. My mind is renewed with positive, almost boundless, energy. A telltale sign that I'm experiencing joy is laughter that's frequently accompanied by tears. (That's why they're called "tears of joy.") Even when joy subsides, its positive effects remain imprinted on my heart and soul. A mysterious goodness has paid me a visit and left behind a different man, slightly better than he was before.

False Happiness, Superficial Happiness

Our world if full of false and shallow versions of happiness that focus exclusively on your material and carnal desires. You chase after personal comfort, pleasure, fun, power, or fame. Wine and dine with the rich and famous. Buy luxury cars. Dress in designer clothing. Buy expensive jewelry. Purchase opulent homes. Throw lavish parties. Buy a big yacht. Purchase a private jet. Go on a more luxurious vacation. Marry a sexier and better looking spouse (without considering his or her character). Sleep around with whomever you fancy, any time you choose. Acquire more toys and more and more things to play with. Seek the approval of moguls, famous celebrities, or powerful politicians.

If you make these things the sole focus of your happiness, you'll be sorely disappointed. They're all superficial substitutes. None of them bring about true happiness. They have no transformative or illuminating power. They're counterfeits. None of them last long enough to truly satisfy you. Oftentimes the more you pursue these things, the emptier and sadder you feel once the initial excitement has worn off.

True happiness is not to be found in entertainment, worldly fame, power, acquiring more things, or pursuing frivolous goals. That is why most of the seemingly "happy" people out there who don't change their ways wind up depressed, miserable, or in rehab. That is why many successful individuals who realize this (sometimes later on in life) shift their focus toward worthy endeavors, admirable works, and charitable causes.

True Happiness (Joy)

Seek happiness for its own sake, and you will not find it;
seek purpose and happiness will follow as a
shadow comes with the sunshine.

—William Scolavino

Search for meaning in your work and your life, and you have laid the foundation for true happiness. Doing meaningful work also prepares us to handle and endure suffering. "Once an individual's search for a meaning is successful, it not only renders him happy but also gives him the capability to cope with suffering," writes Victor E. Frankl.

I have discovered that true happiness is not found when we seek happiness for its own sake. True happiness is the result of living our lives with purpose, accomplishing good things, working hard for what we believe in, and pursuing worthwhile goals and dreams. It arrives most often when we are deeply engaged in doing what we know we should be doing, what our conscience and soul tell us we're meant to do. It also frequently shows up when we're *in the zone*, when we achieve a state of *flow*. We're so absorbed and engaged with our work, that we lose track of time and we experience intense creativity, productivity, and personal fulfillment. Pursuing that kind of happiness is deeply meaningful and satisfying.

Success

Success isn't measured by money or power or social rank.
Success is measured by your discipline and inner peace.
—Mike Ditka

Success is another one of those words that can mean an infinite number of things. Many equate success with power and money. Like fake happiness, superficial success is exclusively focused on making more money and buying more things, on the acquisition of wealth, on gaining more worldly power and influence, or on becoming famous or infamous. That kind of shallow success will always corrupt your character and make you unhappy. Like phony happiness, it will never satisfy you in a deeper sense or bring you peace. It will lead to your destruction in the end. That is not what I mean by *success*.

For me, success means doing what you love and find meaningful; being surrounded by a loving family and genuine friends; getting paid for doing what you're passionate about; earning a comfortable living and having peace in your life; pursuing opportunities that give you more personal and economic freedom; helping others find freedom or discover true happiness (joy) in their lives. Any one of these definitions is preferable to the bogus success peddled by the world. I'm sure your own definition will suffice, once you've thought about it carefully.

Genuine success is the sum of many smaller successes. For example, writing and publishing this book to help you, means *success* to me. All the suffering I have endured and failures I have experienced in my personal and professional life were not in vain. They have produced knowledge and insights that you can use to see the truth, protect yourself, and find meaning in your own struggles. They have resulted in wisdom you can learn from and apply to break free from dysfunctional organizations and improve your life.

Writing this down to share with you has brought great joy

and filled my life with meaning. If it helps you also experience joy and taste true freedom, that will be all the success that I need. Sure, earnings from book sales will be wonderful, the icing on the cake. But financial reward was not my motivation. Money is not the reason why I worked so hard and sacrificed so much to create this book. My love for freedom and the truth, and my passion to help free you, is why I did it. My desire for pursuing what I love to do—to teach, inspire, and motivate others—is why I wrote it. That's my success.

*Your success and happiness lies in you. Resolve to
keep happy, and your joy and you shall form
an invincible host against difficulties.*
—Helen Keller

In your own life and career you will have to define success in terms of what's meaningful and important to you. Please don't buy into the superficial versions of success promoted by shallow celebrities and infamous individuals. They're caricatures of real success. They're fake. Be smart and choose wisely. Your future depends on it.

CHAPTER 4

Pursue Financial, Mental, and Economic Freedom

Everyone needs to strive for financial freedom so that he or she can focus on what he/she loves in life.
—Todd M. Fleming

In the previous chapter we covered the multiple dimensions of freedom. Besides the personal freedoms we benefit from when living and working in a free society, we also need financial, mental, and economic freedom. All of these components are necessary in order for us to experience and maintain our *freedom* in the truest sense of the word. This chapter describes additional freedom components. The definitions are my own unique creations; feel free to use and adjust them to suit your individual lifestyle, risk tolerance, goals, and dreams.

Financial Freedom
You must gain control over your money or the lack of it will forever control you.
—Dave Ramsey

I define *financial freedom* as the ability to be in control of your finances to make the career choices, business decisions, and life choices you want, while paying all your bills, and living comfortably; without getting into trouble financially.

There are different levels of financial freedom that you can achieve. Each level provides you with increasing safety, security, peace of mind, flexibility, and independence. The more money you save and invest, the more personal freedom you can have. All of these levels assume that: (1) you have health insurance coverage, (2) your monthly living expenses are stable and lower than your monthly income, and (3) you have no outstanding credit card debts.

Level 1 – Basic Financial Freedom

You have enough money saved and/or invested in stocks and bonds to cover all your living expenses for at least six months, without receiving a paycheck. Typically this requires saving the equivalent of six months of your current salary.

Level 2 – Solid Financial Freedom

You have enough money saved and/or invested in stocks and bonds, and/or receive additional income from other sources, to cover all your living expenses for at least one year, without receiving a paycheck. This also means that you have saved and invested the cash equivalent of twelve months of your current salary. Mental freedom has arrived. You can quit a job you don't like and follow other opportunities.

Level 3 – Excellent Financial Freedom

You have enough money saved and invested in stocks

and bonds, and/or receive additional income from other investments or sources, and/or earn regular income from a side business, to cover all your living expenses for at least three years, without having to work a regular job. This also means that you have saved and invested the cash equivalent of three years of your current salary. Mental freedom has been firmly established. Your dependency on any one company for your livelihood has significantly decreased. You can easily quit a job you hate, change careers, follow better opportunities, or start your own business.

Level 4 – Superior Financial Freedom

You have enough money saved and invested in stocks and bonds, and receive additional income from multiple other investments or sources, and/or earn regular income from other businesses, to comfortably cover all your living expenses for at least seven years, without having to work a full-time job. This also means that you have saved and invested the cash equivalent of seven years of your current salary. Robust and sustainable wealth has arrived. Economic freedom has been reached. You are no longer dependent on any one company for your livelihood. You can instantly quit your job, change careers, follow better opportunities, start your own business, or pursue what's meaningful to you.

Level 5 – Abundant Financial Freedom

You have more than sufficient money saved and invested in stocks and bonds, and receive additional income from multiple other investments and sources, and earn regular income from multiple other businesses, to comfortably cover all your living expenses for the rest of your life and then some. Robust and sustainable wealth has been achieved. Economic freedom has been firmly established. You never have to work for someone else again. You now have the means to freely pursue what's most meaningful and important to you, for the rest of your life.

If your risk tolerance is higher, it's possible that you'll begin experiencing mental freedom sooner than Level 2. On the other hand, if you're more cautious, you may experience it only when you reach Level 3 or Level 4. Similarly, you may decide that you've attained economic freedom sooner than Level 4, given your experience, resources, or standard of living. If you're more conservative, you may consider Level 5 the point when true economic freedom has been established. Adjust these levels to accommodate your individual tastes, circumstances, needs, and goals. As long at you make consistent and positive progress in the right direction, you're on your way.

How quickly you reach each of these levels will depend on many factors. If you don't have any outstanding debt (besides a mortgage or maybe a car loan) and low monthly expenses, it will allow you to save and invest more money sooner and achieve your goals faster. If you have a lot of debt and high monthly expenses, it will take longer to reach your financial goals. Either way, the sooner you start or accelerate your saving and investing habits, the closer you will be to approaching financial freedom. (For a review or a reminder of key concepts that support financial freedom please read Chapter 5, "Master Financial Freedom Principles.")

Mental Freedom

Financial freedom is freedom from fear.

—Robert Kiyosaki

I identify *mental freedom* as the ability to walk away at anytime from a job you really don't like or an organization that mistreats you. It also allows you to close a business that's no longer profitable or viable, or separate from a troublesome business partner. Mental freedom is a form of spiritual liberty that frees up your mind from anxiety, soul from worry, and heart from fear. It fills your mind and soul with positive energy that boosts your motivation, fuels your passion, and empowers your spirit. It gives you more courage to take calculated risks and follow your dreams.

Reaching some level of financial freedom is a prerequisite to experiencing mental freedom. After all, you need money to support yourself during any transition period. Oftentimes, finding a new job or starting a new business may take a long time. You must have sufficient financial reserves available to pay your bills and have a roof over your head. Money in the bank gives you a measure of safety and security. Without financial resources, worry, anxiety, or fear tend to hang around; and will sap your energy, distract you, and undermine your confidence.

Financial insecurity can even disrupt your job search or entrepreneurial efforts. Others can sense when you're in trouble financially and desperate for money, and will take advantage of you. You may be forced to settle for a lower salary or pay more to get your new business off the ground.

"Take This Job and Shove It" Power

*Freedom means you are unobstructed in living your life
as you choose. Anything less is a form of slavery.*

—Wayne Dyer

Mental freedom helps you endure a less than ideal current job situation and cope more effectively with a manipulative or nasty boss. It allows you to quit at any moment; you gain "take this job and shove it" power. You're now in better control of your destiny. Frustrating work conditions won't affect you as much as they did before. Incompetence and idiocy that used to drive you crazy no longer matter. Aggravations caused by office politics will roll off your back; it becomes much easier to ignore them. Even your obnoxious manager won't seem as bothersome as before.

When things get rough at work you can exercise your mental freedom to escape psychologically. It allows you to daydream. You can envision a new path for your life and plan your exit. You can channel your frustration and anger into positive and constructive energy to prepare for a better future and explore other options. Knowing that you won't have to put up with this kind of nonsense much longer is incredibly liberating. You no longer feel trapped. This will only be temporary. You don't feel powerless anymore. You have the means and ability to escape. You have hope. When you're ready, you can quit and pursue your freedom and happiness elsewhere.

The financial and mental freedom I achieved—after many years of rigorous financial discipline, hard work, and careful planning—allowed me to say *no* to those sociopathic individuals, toxic companies, and dysfunctional universities that mistreated and took advantage of me. These freedoms gave me the confidence to turn down work that was not aligned with my goals and dreams. These two freedoms gradually liberated my mind and gave me more time to say *yes* to what I'm truly passionate about and love to do. This book, 15 years in the making, finally became a reality due to deliberate long-term financial planning, consistent effort, and many short-term sacrifices during those same 15 years.

Self-Confidence Boost

Self-confidence is linked to almost every element involved in a happy and fulfilling life.
—Barbara Markway

Increased self-confidence is an important side-effect of attaining a reasonable level of financial and mental freedom. It infuses you with positive energy, motivates you to act and take concrete steps toward your most important goals. Tangible results fuel your self-confidence, energizing you to take even more steps in the right direction. You have created a positive feedback loop to help you reach economic freedom.

Greater confidence gives you courage to stand up for yourself and can improve your workplace situation. When others see and sense your newfound confidence, they respond differently. They may not figure out what's going on, but they'll definitely notice that you're more relaxed, happy, and self-assured. You'll have a new "don't mess with me" spring in your step. You'll project an "I don't care anymore" attitude. Your co-workers may even show you more respect.

Self-confidence signals to troublesome co-workers and abusive bosses that you're not a pushover. They may start to back off when they notice you're no longer influenced or intimidated by their tactics. Even if they won't change their ways, at least they will avoid confronting or bothering you as often. You'll have more breathing room and quiet time to yourself; freeing up more energy to invest in reaching your ultimate goal, economic freedom. Plus, you'll have many healthy chuckles at the puzzled looks and frowns of your confused boss when he realizes that his manipulative schemes and threats no longer work on you.

Economic Freedom

The goal isn't more money.
The goal is living life on your terms.

—Will Rogers

Economic independence is a pre-requisite and necessary companion to achieving true and lasting liberty, for being free in the truest sense of the word. *Economic freedom* is reached when your financial freedom and mental freedom have provided you with the necessary wealth and diverse income streams—from multiple investments and busi-nesses—to comfortably cover all your living expenses for the rest of your life and still have enough money left over to pur-sue any other meaningful endeavor you desire, without having to work for anyone else again. You have achieved robust and sustainable prosperity. You can now live life on your terms.

Economic freedom also gives you back time, a most pre-cious and irreplaceable commodity. Your financial independence frees up your time to spend on the most impor-tant things in your life: your family and friends, your health, your hobbies, your life mission, or anything else you are passionate about and enjoy doing. You have reached a level of safety and security where genuine freedom and happiness (joy) can thrive. You can now taste the full effect of liberty. You're experiencing freedom in all its glorious and blessed aspects.

CHAPTER 5

Master Financial Freedom Principles

You do pay a price for your financial freedom, but it is far lesser than what you pay for a lifetime of slavery.
—Manoj Arora

Make your finances and investments a top priority. If you have a good handle on your money and overall financial situation, then you should further develop and sharpen financial discipline and rigor, so you can meet your goals and achieve financial freedom sooner. If you have already mastered the financial concepts and guidance covered in this chapter, and have reached superior or abundant financial freedom, then feel free to skip it.

There are no shortcuts, no legitimate *get-rich-quick* formulas, to attaining true financial and economic freedom. Achieving financial independence comes at a price; but it's a price worth paying to gain your freedom. It requires constant learning, sacrifices, focus, discipline, vigilance, and patience. You have to practice these skills continually and consistently. You have to give them time to work. This is a long distance marathon, not a sprint. The good news is that time is your friend. The power of diversification and compound interest will accelerate your efforts. Savings and investments earn interest, then you earn more interest on that interest. The sooner you start saving and investing, the better off you will be in the long term.

Fundamental Financial Principles

The understanding and utilization of money have gone a revolutionary change over the decades. Hence from an early life do not let your finances be handled by advisors or your bank. Rather read yourself and try to gain the knowledge about the dynamics of money and its investments.
—Sachin Mittal

To achieve financial and economic freedom become familiar and comfortable with financial and investment principles. You don't need to become a banker or a Wall Street financial expert, but you ought to achieve a solid level of understanding and competency when managing and investing your money. Otherwise, you risk making serious mistakes that will undermine your financial condition or lead to catastrophic monetary losses. You've heard the old expression, "a fool and his money are soon parted." It's true. It happens all the time. Please, don't be that fool. Educate yourself and learn to be smart with your money, careful with your budget, and wise with your investments. These are life-long skills to learn and apply. They will guide you, help you, protect you, and eventually lead you to financial security and independence.

There are several fundamental principles, financial *dos* and *don'ts*, that you should follow to maximize your ability to reach financial freedom, acquire mental freedom, and earn economic freedom. These concepts are similar to strategies that other financial experts and successful individuals recommend for achieving financial independence and personal prosperity. While the financial guidance in this chapter is thorough, it is by no means complete. I cover broad financial and investment guidelines for you to consider and use. They have worked well for me. Fine-tune them as needed to address your individual situation and circumstances.

Financial Freedom Dos

It is what a person will do with the saved money that will make a big difference in his or her finances.
—H. J. Chammas

Here are several important financial freedom principles to always keep in mind and adopt:

1. **Budget and track all your expenses and income.** Keep track of your expenses and income every month. Start right away. Use any electronic spreadsheet or financial budgeting program that provides you with the necessary tools and functionality to monitor all your expenses and income. Check your financial condition on a regular basis (every month, at a minimum), stay within your budget, and don't overspend.

2. **Balance your accounts and verify all charges.** Balance your checking and savings accounts, and reconcile them with your bank account statements every month. Check that everything matches. Keep all your receipts (printed or electronic versions) for all your purchases or online

transactions; using your credit or debit card, or other electronic payments. Save emails with order notifications and amounts spent for anything ordered online. Review all credit card statements and compare against all charges. Use your receipts and match them with the detailed credit card reports or bank statements. Investigate and resolve any discrepancies or mistakes. Do this every month. Be consistent. If you wait too long, it will be harder to reverse incorrect charges or fraudulent transactions.

3. **Spend less than you earn.** This is an important rule of life. Your expenses should be less than your income. Reduce all unnecessary expenses. It's the best way to start saving and laying the foundation of your financial security and freedom. Immediately reduce expenses if they are equal to or greater than your income. Be thorough and creative in finding ways to cut costs and save money.

4. **Increase your income.** If you have downsized and cut spending as much as possible but your expenses are still too high, explore additional opportunities to earn more money: work overtime (if it's compensated), try to get a raise in your current position, get a second part-time job, look for consulting work, start a side business, or find other (legal) ways to increase your income. Do whatever it takes to start saving money on a regular basis.

5. **Save, Save, Save.** Save as much money as you can, as often as you can. Start saving as soon as possible and continue saving for the rest of your life. As a minimum, save at least 10% of your monthly salary and other earned income. Aim to eventually save 20-25% each month. This may take time, but be patient and stay focused—the re-

wards far outweigh the sacrifices. If you cannot save at least 10% now, then start with 5%, 3%, 2%, or 1% of each paycheck (or even $20 or $50 a month, if that's all you can afford), then gradually increase it once you get your finances under control and become comfortable with the process.

6. **Pay off your credit cards in full every month.** Use your credit cards only as interest-free short-term loans. Pay off the balances in full each month. Pay careful attention to what you spend to make sure you can cover 100% of the amounts due in each pay cycle.

7. **Pay off all outstanding debts.** Most credit card debts require you to pay excessively high interest rates, much higher than any interest rates you can earn on savings or return on stocks and bonds investments. Therefore, pay down and eliminate those high-interest debts as soon as possible, before you start saving. It's counterproductive to pay 15-20% interest on outstanding credit card balances while you earn 2-3% interest on your savings. (Your home mortgage, car loan, or student loans should be the only exceptions to this rule.)

8. **Start your retirement plan as soon as possible.** Many organizations offer employees company-sponsored retirement accounts with some level of matching contributions. Known as 401(k) plans, these accounts allow employees to contribute, pre-tax, a portion of their paychecks. Larger employers then match part of that contribution amount up to a certain percentage (typically 5%) towards your retirement balance.

For example, let's assume your company does a 5%

match. If you setup a 5% salary deduction for your 401(k) account, your employer will also contribute 5% of your paycheck every pay period. Ten percent of your salary (your 5% + company matching 5%) goes into your 401(k) account, tax free. You immediately get a 100% return on your retirement savings. Better still, 401(k) contributions are done from your gross salary, before federal and state income taxes are deducted. This means you get to keep more of your hard-earned money in your retirement account, helping it grow faster. Additionally, your 401(k) contributions also reduce your taxable income for that year. (Please check with your company's HR department and a retirement specialist to insure you maximize this benefit and setup your 401(k) plan correctly.)

9. **Beat inflation, invest in stocks and bonds.** As the cost of living goes up and prices increase (inflation), the purchasing power of your cash decreases. The same amount of cash can buy fewer things. Using only money market or certificate of deposit accounts for your savings is not enough to keep up with inflation, especially after you pay taxes on the interest earned. The low interest rates offered by these financial products are insufficient to protect the market value of your money. "Today people who hold cash equivalents feel comfortable. They shouldn't. They have opted for a terrible long-term asset, one that pays virtually nothing and is certain to depreciate in value," cautions successful billionaire investor Warren Buffett.

You will need to invest a certain percentage of your savings in stocks, bonds, mutual funds, index funds, or other types of market funds. These investments are riskier, but they earn greater returns over the long term. This is the only way to keep up with and beat inflation, and maximize the purchasing power of your money. (Please use those money management books I recommended earlier to better grasp and master these concepts, or seek the expert advice of trusted and reputable financial advisors—never listen to just one.)

10. **Diversify your investments intelligently.** Practice the old adage: "don't put all your eggs in one basket." Never put all your money into the shares of one company or into a single investment. Intelligently diversify your investments (stocks, bonds, mutual funds) so you have a good asset mix and balance out the overall risks. Don't buy different stocks just for the sake of diversification. Carefully research and know exactly what you're buying, before diversifying your investment portfolio. Make sure you understand the fundamentals of those businesses and the industries in which they operate. Look for undiscovered value and companies that have solid potential for future growth, corporations that others have overlooked. This is how Warren Buffett built his massive fortune: "I make no attempt to forecast the market—my efforts are devoted to finding undervalued securities."

11. **Stay in control of your money and investments.** Maintain full control and ownership of all your money, stocks, bonds, and all other investments. Never give someone else, except perhaps your spouse, ownership or control over your bank accounts, stock trading accounts, retirement accounts, or any other investment accounts.

12. **Track and gradually increase your net worth.** Keep track of your personal net worth, as you regularly monitor

your income and expenses. Your individual net worth is the difference between all your assets (cash, investments, real estate, personal property, etc.) and all your liabilities, your debts (home mortgage, car loan, student loans, credit card debt, other debts). Your first goal is to reach a positive net worth. Then aim to steadily increase your net worth every year. Checking that information will be easier once you proactively start tracking your income, expenses, and investments. It can be invigorating and reassuring to see your net worth grow as you make progress toward your financial and economic freedom.

13. **You're never too old to start.** There is no such thing as being too old to focus on your financial health and pursue financial freedom. No one enjoys scraping by and being constantly worried about paying bills, whether you're 25 or 75. Relying solely on a measly Social Security check will not be enough to live comfortably in retirement. Picture yourself being 75 and still having to work a part-time or full-time job to cover your expenses and avoid losing your house; or being forced to move into a tiny apartment in a bad neighborhood so you can afford your rent.

Worse still, imagine being 75 years old, having to work to survive and reporting every day to an obnoxious and arrogant 25-year-old manager who bosses you around. Use these awful scenarios as motivation to act now, get your finances in order, and plan for a more secure future. Start today and do everything possible to improve your financial situation to avoid a dismal outcome. Channel your fear of failure into positive energy to steel your resolve and motivate yourself into action.

14. **Give it time.** Be patient. "The stock market is a device to transfer money from the impatient to the patient," reminds us Warren Buffett. Time is your friend. Give these principles time to work. Remember, this is a marathon, not a sprint. Stay on course and continually focus on the long-term results. Achieving even a little bit of financial freedom will build up your confidence and inspire you to keep going in the right direction. Envision how rewarding it will be to taste more of that liberty. Continue to strive toward that goal, it will be worth it.

Financial Freedom Don'ts

The speed of your success is limited only by your dedication and what you're willing to sacrifice.
—Nathan W. Morris

Listed below are bad habits that you need to avoid in order to maximize your chances of reaching financial freedom:

1. **Don't live paycheck to paycheck.** This is the flip side of save, save, save. Unfortunately, a vast majority of Americans live paycheck to paycheck. They spend all they earn and then wait anxiously for the next paycheck to arrive. Numerous surveys also show that almost half of U.S. households have less than $500 in savings. This is surviving, not living or thriving. No wonder so many people are unhappy. Move away from this detrimental cycle. Use the advice provided in this chapter and in this book to get started as soon as possible.

2. **Don't overspend or spend impulsively.** Don't buy things you cannot afford. Don't spend money on discre-

tionary (non-essential) items like premium brands, luxury products, designer clothing, jewelry, entertainment, fine dining, vacations, cruises, concerts, or any other recreational activities, when your current income cannot cover or support such purchases. Discretionary spending is ok if you don't have any credit card debt, you're already saving at least 10% of your income every paycheck, you have sufficient additional income available to afford it, and you can pay for it in full—without using up your savings or accumulating credit card debt.

3. **Don't accumulate credit card debt.** Don't use credit cards for purchases when you cannot pay off their full balances by the next due date. Credit cards charge very high interest rates on all unpaid balances. Those large interest payments will dramatically increase the outstanding credit card debt that you owe. As total balances rapidly escalate, you will fall further and further behind in your quest to establish financial freedom. You also risk insolvency and bankruptcy, which will ruin your credit score and make it that much more difficult to get your finances in order.

4. **Don't buy things to put on appearances.** Don't buy status symbol items to impress others or pretend you're someone you're not. Don't do anything to promote a false image of yourself and hurt your financial situation. Don't buy a new car every few years. Don't buy a bigger house than you can afford. Fleeting positive emotions should not dictate your purchases. Regret, anxiety, and frustration will appear instead when you're in trouble financially, work for a boss or company that mistreats you, and cannot quit your job because of your poor finan-

cial situation. You'll feel much worse and be that much further away from freedom and genuine happiness.

5. **Don't take on unnecessary debt.** Don't borrow money to invest in an unproven venture or a sketchy investment you hear about from an acquaintance, see on TV, or learn about in an infomercial. Don't take out a second mortgage on your house to renovate your home because it's "too dated," or spend that money on non-essential things. Second mortgages should be used only in extreme conditions or emergency situations; for example, to pay for critical medical procedures.

6. **Don't put all your eggs in one basket.** Never invest all your savings into a single stock, bond, corporation, mutual fund, or any other single investment; no matter how large the potential rate of return could be and how many "guarantees" you're promised. It's extremely risky and dangerous. (For effective diversification strategies, please reference the *financial dos* list above.)

7. **Don't invest in anything you don't understand.** "Never invest in a business you cannot understand," warns Warren Buffett. Don't put money into a venture you know nothing about or barely comprehend. That would be gambling, not investing. Take the time to learn and understand exactly what you're buying into. Thoroughly evaluate the actual value, potential risks and rewards, and realistic long-term prospects of each business, venture, stock, bond, security, fund, trust, or any other investment you are considering.

8. **Don't let your emotions influence financial or investment decisions.** Subjective feelings should not form the

basis of your financial strategies or investment decisions. Emotional biases and unreasonable apprehensions can negatively influence your choices, lead to poor decision-making, and cause unnecessary financial losses. Never make decisions when you're either angry, in a bad mood, anxious, or depressed. Don't panic and make decisions based on fear. Be careful when you're overly enthusiastic or feel irrationally exuberant. Impulse buying is fine in an ice cream shop, but disastrous on Wall Street. Emotional lows and highs can precipitate rash financial actions that you'll regret later. "Once you have ordinary intelligence, what you need is the temperament to control the urges that get other people into trouble in investing," advises Warren Buffett. Use your cool intellect and reason to make logical financial decisions that are focused on long-term growth. All your evaluations, calculations, and assessments need to be grounded in reality. Rely on solid data and accurate information to conduct an objective analysis.

9. **Don't gamble on any "sure thing" investments.** Stay away from anyone who promises very large or outlandish "guaranteed" or "safe" returns on an investment. If it sounds too good to be true, then it isn't true. All financial investments that earn more than the average risk-free rate—typically offered by certificate of deposit or money market accounts—are never safe. And each of those accounts are only safe because the Federal Deposit Insurance Corporation (FDIC) insures them up to a certain amount. All investments besides FDIC-insured bank accounts have some level of risk. And the higher the rate of return these investments promise, the greater the risk

of loss. Even U.S. Treasury Bills (T-Bills) carry the risk of the U.S. federal government defaulting. Yes, the likelihood of the American government defaulting on its debt service obligations is relatively small, but it's still not zero. Don't forget that!

10. **Don't depend on only one financial advisor.** Find unbiased financial advisors and investment specialists who have your best interests in mind and charge reasonable fees. Use them for expert guidance and additional suggestions, but also do your own research and educate yourself thoroughly about financial issues and investment options. Never follow the advice of only one specific advisor, consult with at least a couple of specialists and validate their recommendations. Verify that they have no conflicts of interest that can affect their impartiality or influence the advice they provide.

11. **Don't follow the crowd.** Never do something simply because everyone else is doing it. Don't change your financial strategies because it's suddenly trendy or popular to invest in certain companies or industries. Don't be influenced by some celebrity spokesperson or self-proclaimed market guru claiming to predict the future or the "next big thing." Adhere to solid financial concepts and fundamental investment principles, and focus on value, growth, and long-term results, regardless of the short-term noise, frenzy, or hysteria.

The following advice from Warren Buffett, the most successful investor in the world (net worth of approximately $79 billion as of 2020), perfectly encapsulate this exact concept:

- "You are neither right nor wrong because the crowd disagrees with you. You are right because your data and reasoning are right."

- "Don't get caught up with what other people are doing. Being a contrarian isn't the key but being a crowd follower isn't either. You need to detach yourself emotionally."

- "Most people get interested in stocks when everyone else is. The time to get interested is when no one else is. You can't buy what is popular and do well."

- "Those who invest only when commentators are upbeat end up paying a heavy price for meaningless reassurance."

Other Books to Help You

Remember that there are many financial planning, money management, and investment advice books and resources out there. They cover comparable concepts and information, but in greater detail. I highly recommend reading a few of them. Invest your time and efforts in this process; it will pay dividends in the long term. If you haven't read any good books on these topics, please research at least two different books—check the reviews and pick the best ones—and buy them as soon as possible. Always preview the table of contents to see what each book covers. I suggest that you read several excerpts or a few chapters of each book, to insure they're well-written and clear, easy to read and follow, and compatible with your learning style. Once you have these books in hand, read and use them for your benefit.

CHAPTER 6

Leadership Principles are Universal

*It is human beings, not space aliens, who work and
interact daily in all these organizations.
They are the same as you and me.*

When the term "organization" is used throughout this book, it
can refer to a business, company, or corporation; school, college, or university; religious or non-profit organization;
government, law enforcement, or social service agency; the
military; or any other type of private foundation or public
institution—either for profit or non-profit—where people
work and are compensated for their time and efforts. Similarly, when you see "business," "company," or "corporation"
it can mean any organization or institution, public or private.

Why cast such a wide net? Because, leadership principles
are universal. They apply to people in every organization,
across cultures and countries. It's only leadership practices
that may be adjusted to fit the unique characteristics of an
organization or local customs.

For example, "recognizing and rewarding employees" is a
principle. How each organization implements that is a practice. Some companies do it with balloons and cash bonuses,

some with plaques and additional vacation time, and others with cakes and gift cards. In each instance the principle is applied correctly, only the practice changes to suit the uniqueness of the culture and the employees who work there.

Human Beings Work Here
When people go to work, they shouldn't have to leave their hearts at home.
—Betty Bender

Message to managers and executives across all organizations: "You live and work on planet Earth and manage real people, start acting that way!"

Human beings, not space aliens, work and interact daily in all companies and organizations. They are the same as you and me. They are men and women of flesh and blood. They have hearts, minds, and souls. They have hopes, dreams, and desires. They're imperfect. They have hang-ups, apprehensions, and fears. They feel physical and psychological pain. They search for meaning in their lives and careers. They seek to belong. They want to be appreciated, respected, and recognized. They want to be treated fairly. They want to know that they matter, that their managers genuinely care about them as individuals, that their organizations value their efforts and contributions.

Employees don't stop being human when they work for a university, government agency, or a non-profit foundation. The laws of economics, the dynamics of human relationships, ethical and leadership principles, equity and fairness rules, human motivation theories, and reality and truth don't suddenly change or stop working when you're employed by the government or an academic institution. I believe the reason why these organizations are so badly and incompetently managed is because those in charge have forgotten, never learned, or purposely ignore this fundamental truth. Or they simply don't care about the people who "work for them."

The Problem: Dysfunctional and Hypocritical Managers

Clueless and dysfunctional managers seem to think that leadership and economic concepts do not have universal application. That somehow individuals who work in their organizations are different and don't care so much about money, fairness, meaning, personal fulfillment, accountability, recognition, and professional growth. This is nonsense. It's simply not true. This mentality has lead to catastrophic results in many workplaces. It has allowed individuals to masquerade as managers and leaders while doing the exact opposite of what they're supposed to do. No wonder most employees have either lost hope or given up. This is not how it's supposed to be. These are not leaders, they're impostors. They undermine the success of their organizations and crush the spirit of their employees.

Astoundingly, most of those individuals in management and leadership positions have academic degrees: bachelor's, master's, and doctorates. They have studied and supposedly learned world-class principles of how to lead and treat employees. They should know exactly how to strategically manage companies and organizations. However, once they reach positions of power and influence, most of that formal education seems to go out the window. Little, if any of it, is practiced or applied in the workplace.

Even university professors, faculty chairs, associate deans, deans, and administrators with doctorates in business, management, education, or leadership fail to practice what they learned and continue to teach their students. Many don't practice what they preach and teach. Rarely do they apply any of it in dealing with subordinates or colleagues on campus. While they continue to publish all sorts of academic research and articles on the best ways to lead and motivate employees, they themselves manage human beings poorly, even abusively. While they criticize corporations and executives for acting unethically and mistreating employees, they act the same. This is hypocritical in the extreme. They behave worse than business owners and managers who lack university degrees or PhDs in management or leadership.

The Solution: Men and Women of Character and Integrity

Organizations need honorable and trustworthy leaders who consistently put into practice great leadership principles, not merely talk or philosophize about them. Companies need men and women of character and integrity—in all senior executive positions and management roles—who have the courage and conviction to lead wisely.

In fact, I have met wonderful leaders and amazing business owners with only high school diplomas. These self-taught men and women have extensive real-world experience. They display exemplary leadership skills. They have character and integrity. They're decent and kind human beings. They walk their talk and lead by example. They apply human-centered leadership principles better than many corporate executives with MBAs or college deans with PhDs from reputable universities. These genuine leaders treat their employees with more compassion, decency, and fairness than you'd find in most company boardrooms or come across on many university campuses. These men and women of character easily build trust, inspire loyalty, and foster strong workplace relationships. They are the solution!

CHAPTER 7

The Three Most Important Rules in Business

Follow these three rules consistently, and your business will remain healthy and profitable for the long term. It will prosper and thrive. Ignore them, and failure is sure to follow.

This foundational chapter covers essential rules of business, profitability, wealth creation, and leadership. These concepts encapsulate business acumen that should be universally considered and practiced by business owners and leaders of any organization. These rules will inevitably lead to sustainable profitability, healthy growth, and real long-term success.

Use this information to compare and contrast with what's going on in your organization or business. Observe whether managers and executives practice these principles. In my experience, many companies either partially ignore or completely fail to implement one or more of these fundamental rules, all the time. Assess if management would be open and willing to consider these ideas and actually apply them. Strive to practice these rules in your workplace, if it's possible and reasonable to do so.

Reference these fundamental rules when evaluating companies for potential investment opportunities. As covered in the previous chapter, before buying stock in any corporation conduct research to accurately assess its condition and better understand what you're buying into. You can gain critical insights and make a more informed decision when you evaluate how well a company applies these three rules.

Finally, apply these principles in your own venture or side business to give yourself the best chance of success. Follow these three rules consistently, and your business will remain healthy and profitable for the long term. It will prosper and thrive. Ignore them, and failure is sure to follow.

Listed below are the three rules I have developed. They encompass knowledge and insights that other experts, successful entrepreneurs, and influential business leaders have also advocated; although they may have worded or prioritized them differently.

Rule #1 – Always Meet and Exceed Customer Expectations

The key is to set realistic customer expectations, and then not to just meet them, but to exceed them—preferably in unexpected and helpful ways.

—Richard Branson

Meeting and exceeding customer expectations is the most important but often overlooked rule of business. A company will stay in business only if its customers are satisfied and happy with the product(s) or service(s) it offers. This generates profits, builds a strong brand, supports customer loyalty, and builds long-term stability and success. It's also the best way to deal with existing competitors and fend off future new entrants in the marketplace. Meeting expectations should be the baseline for company performance. Exceeding expectations is the ultimate goal.

The best way for a business to exceed its customers' expectations is by providing real value for the price asked in exchange. When consumers purchase a product or service and believe they have received something worthwhile in return, baseline expectations have been met. When customers maintain that perspective weeks, months, or years later, the company is well on its way toward exceeding expectations. A sure-fire sign that expectations are exceeded is the consumers' willingness to pay extra for a company's products or services, despite lower prices or extra features offered by competitors. Customers reviews and feedback also indicate if a business meets and exceeds its customers' expectations.

Small Businesses

Typically small businesses, who compete against bigger and more established companies, practice this rule far better than their larger competitors. These smaller companies tend to stay closer to their customers and pay careful attention to their concerns and needs. Their customer service is top notch and more responsive. These businesses understand that every contact with a client influences whether or not that customer will return. If they do not deliver excellence, they will lose customers. In turn, superior customer service builds trust and strengthens consumer loyalty, helping to differentiate these businesses from direct and indirect competitors.

Virtually all of the small businesses our family and friends frequent follow this rule. Their employees always strive to meet and exceed our expectations. They treat us like human beings, not just numbers or things to be exploited for cash.

We enjoy their products and services, and trust their owners and employees. We appreciate their personalized and responsive customer service. Unsurprisingly, these companies have nearly perfect online reviews and consistently receive glowing feedback from their customers. Word-of-mouth is their most effective form of marketing and advertising. All of these companies were enthusiastically referred to us by close friends and trusted family members, or we picked them ourselves based on the stellar reviews of their current customers. We, in turn, have also enthusiastically recommended these businesses to others.

Large Corporations

Quite a few large corporations seem to have abandoned this rule; their senior executives don't seem to care. This is confirmed by my own experiences and reflected in the online reviews and feedback from millions of consumers. These companies typically have average, poor, or dreadful reviews from their customers. I depend on several of these billion-dollar organizations because of their market dominance or due to lack of viable alternatives. They include companies like Ebay, Google, Microsoft, PayPal, Facebook, and Blackboard. I remain a user or a customer because I have no choice, not because I like their products or services, or appreciate their customer service. The moment a feasible competitor appears that can deliver the functionality and responsiveness I need at a reasonable price, I will instantly abandon any of these companies, never to return.

When people call our call center, our reps don't have scripts, and they don't try to up-sell. They are just

judged on whether they go above and beyond for the customer and really deliver a kind of personal service and emotional connection with our customers.
—Tony Hsieh

There are some remarkable large businesses who follow this rule consistently. Companies like Costco, USAA, Amazon, Southwest Airlines, and Zappos are brilliant at meeting and exceeding their customers' expectations. This is substantiated by millions of happy customers and the success of these organizations. Unfortunately, these companies are the rare exceptions. There's a lot of room for improvement in other corporations. Those entrepreneurs and business owners who capitalize on this oversight and consistently practice this rule will reap the rewards the marketplace has to offer; those who don't, won't.

If you already own your own business or plan to eventually launch a new venture, aim to be one of those individuals who always practices rule #1. Also, if your current managers are willing to listen and change, you might be able to convince them to adopt or follow this rule more closely. Remind them of the financial windfalls that will follow, if they still need convincing.

Rule #2 – Work to Build Long-Term Profitability and Increased Long-Term Value of the Business

Chasing profits and building a long-term profit model are two different things.
—Lewis Howes

A company needs to earn a healthy return to be successful and prosper. If a business cannot create value and achieve long-term profitability, it should close. It's pointless to risk money, time, energy, and resources to break even or lose money. It would be better for that money to be invested elsewhere and earn a reasonable profit; meanwhile the freed up time and resources could be used for another viable endeavor.

Legitimate profitability (as opposed to *destructive profitability*) enhances the long-term value, growth, and competitiveness of an enterprise. It is achieved when business owners and executives maintain a long-term perspective and create sustainable long-term profitability that boosts a company's net worth. Legitimate profitability is best achieved through strategic long-term planning, disciplined action, continual improvements, and constant innovation. Real value is created for shareholders, customers, and employees.

When a business practices rule #1 and commits to meeting and exceeding customer needs consistently, then legitimate profitability can be achieved. Employees are critical in this process and should be treated and compensated accordingly, as we'll see with rule #3. After all, they're the ones who interact with and take care of the customers. Employees are the face and heart of any business.

To maintain legitimate profitability a long-term perspective is required for all management actions. Everything the company does in the short-term needs to fully align with and support long-term strategies that reinforce healthy profitability and value creation. Short-term decisions cannot undermine or conflict with a company's long-term objectives, no matter how profitable they appear in the moment. As a matter of fact, concentrating solely on misaligned short-term objectives while ignoring long-term consequences is a recipe for certain failure.

Destructive Profitability:
Excessive Short-Term Focus

Good management has nothing to do with short-term successes and the management elixirs that allegedly led to them....It cannot be achieved by judgments based on quarterly results, but rather emerges from a deeply rooted understanding of the durable, unclouded by short-term spectacular success stories.

—Hermann Simon

Unfortunately, many corporate executives and business owners embrace a form of *destructive profitability* that endangers a company's future. They sacrifice product or service quality, customer satisfaction, brand value, and employee morale through an excessive preoccupation with fast results, cost-cutting, and short-term profitability. They operate in a perpetual "profits now, forget about tomorrow" mode. Customer expectations are rarely considered. Building trust with consumers is the last thing on the mind of management. Employees are often treated as objects to be used and discarded at will, without any thought that they're human beings, not furniture or computer equipment.

Poor customer service is typically an accurate sign of an organization's shortsightedness. Customer service is treated as a burden or a chore; the company reluctantly provides it, but it's given low priority and minimal resources. Customer support is frequently outsourced to third-party providers with representatives who read from scripts and lack sufficient experience to quickly assist customers. Companies also install those insufferable automated phone systems that force consumers to jump through ridiculous hoops to finally talk to a human being and get some help.

An excessive reliance on cost-cutting measures and outsourcing strategies—without regard to their impact on customer experiences—negatively affects customer and employee satisfaction, jeopardizes the company's brand, decreases overall value, and undermines the company's ability to achieve sustained future growth. Yet, compensation packages, bonus mechanisms, and promotion criteria reward executives for short-term results and encourage them to stay focused primarily on the present. Unethical and selfish managers have no reason to change. This myopic approach weakens the company, alienates customers and employees, and eventually destroys the business.

Rule #3 – Treat Your Employees the Same Way You Expect Them to Treat Your Best Customers

Every one of your team members is important and worthy of care. Every one of them is instrumental in the future of your business, and your business should be instrumental in their lives.
—Bob Chapman

Employees are critical for the long-term success and survivability of any company. Without them, the first two important rules in business will not operate effectively and consistently. No organization can thrive without top-notch employees and people-focused leadership strategies and processes. Leaders need to recruit and hire the right people and best individuals for each business.

Transforming, if possible, all existing employees into their best employees is another management responsibility. This does not mean that everyone will have the same experience, education, skills, and performance abilities. It does mean, that all employees should be the best at what they do. Their personalities should fit the organizational culture. It also means that their knowledge and abilities match their positions, functional roles, and the actual work employees perform daily.

Get the Right People on the Bus

In his book, *Good to Great*, Jim Collins called the process of hiring the most suitable employees "getting the right people on the bus." Collins and his team of researchers examined hundreds of companies across many different industries and conclusively proved that having the right employees is *the* distinguishing characteristic that helps good businesses become great enterprises. "The executives who ignited the transformations from good to great did not first figure out where to drive the bus and then get people to take it there. No, they first got the right people on the bus (and the wrong people off the bus) and then figured out where to drive it," observes Collins.

Management is responsible for establishing and promoting a culture that does not tolerate incompetent, irresponsible, lazy, or unqualified employees. Those individuals who don't meet the required performance criteria for their positions should be mentored, helped, and given an opportunity to improve, within a reasonable amount of time. If no improvement is forthcoming, management has to let them go and hire employees who can do the job and will put in the effort.

The tremendous value, ingenuity, and resourcefulness only human beings can offer, are more reasons why companies need to actively recruit, promote, and hold on to excellent employees. "Machinery can increase productivity in measurable increments, and new processes can create significant efficiencies. However, only people can stun you with quantum leaps. Only people can do ten times what even they thought they could. Only people can exceed your wildest dreams, and only people can make you feel great at the end of the day. Everything we consider valuable in life and business begins and ends with people," asserts Bob Chapman.

Chapman is absolutely right. Employees are an organization's most valuable and precious resources. Only people can insure that customers' expectations are always met and exceeded, which supports legitimate long-term profitability and value creation. Only the human mind can deliver astonishing innovation, creativity, and productivity. Only people can maintain the competitiveness and protect the longevity of an organization. Only people can transform good businesses into extraordinary and successful enterprises.

Non-Business Settings – Other Organizations

What about organizations that are not businesses with customers or operate in a not-for-profit mode? Can these rules apply in those institutions? Yes, as a matter of fact they can and should operate as well. After all, people work there (employees) and other human beings are typically the beneficiaries (customers) of the efforts of those same organizations.

Rules #1 and #3 will work with some adjustments, to insure they function properly. For rule #1, management will have to design accurate techniques that capture and measure the satisfaction of the people the organization helps (the equivalent of "customer expectations"). For rule #3, organizations will need to create objective methods to measure employee productivity (unique to each workplace) and implement effective processes to fairly recognize and proportionally reward employees based on their individual performance.

Rule #2 will be somewhat more difficult to implement since profitability is not a factor in not-for-profit organizations. Here's where human ingenuity and creativity will help. With rule #3 firmly established, management will have great employees who can brainstorm and give innovative feedback on how to properly apply rule #2. Managers and employees can collaboratively design comparable organizational performance benchmarks (unique to each institution) that substitute for profitability and value. These new benchmarks can then be used to track the overall operational efficiency and effectiveness of the organization, and support its long-term success.

Yes, it does sound idealistic. Given the dysfunctional reality in many not-for-profit organizations, public institutions, and government agencies this approach seems almost impossible. Hard? Yes. Difficult? Yes. Impossible? No. Due to the entrenched cultures in these workplaces bringing about change will be incredibly difficult. I never claimed this was going to be easy. However, these three rules work and can deliver superior results. Their application can significantly improve the status quo, if management has the courage and conviction to implement them.

Practicing the Three Rules

Based on the multiple benefits and large profit potential these three rules can produce, you would think that management would rush to implement them and never deviate from following them. Unfortunately, experience has shown that only a few companies practice all three rules properly; many barely practice two or even one; and some practice none at all. Is it any wonder why we're so often disappointed and frustrated as customers, and discouraged and demotivated as employees?

CHAPTER 8

Live in Reality, Seek the Truth

*The truth does not change according
to our ability to stomach it.*
—Flannery O'Connor

*To see what is in front of one's nose
needs a constant struggle.*
—George Orwell

Everything we do in our lives must be grounded in *truth*. We need to see reality as it really is and see ourselves as we truly are. We have to be hardcore realists. Why? Because, as I explained in a previous chapter, truth and freedom are inseparably linked; unless they co-exist, true freedom can never be attained.

Staying grounded in truth demands constant learning, hard work, and discipline. Living in reality requires grit and determination. It assumes we're willing to hear the truth and change. It compels us to be humble and teachable. It forces us to admit mistakes and make the necessary changes quickly. It demands that we "keep it real" 24 hours a day, seven days a week.

What is Truth?

Truth is an external condition of what is real. It is
independent of human interpretation.
It has its own objective reality.
—Bill Whittle

What exactly is "truth"? We live in a world where *truth* is frequently ignored and gradually redefined out of existence. It's increasingly confused with subjective opinions or feelings. "That is *your* truth. *My* truth is different." Many even claim that there's no truth at all, that truth does not exist. "The truth is just a human invention. It's just a figment of your imagination. You cannot know the truth."

A simple and clear definition of *truth* comes from Bill Whittle: "Truth is an external condition of what is real. It is independent of human interpretation. It has its own objective reality." If we get this right, then everything else that follows has a chance for success. If we don't, then we're in serious trouble and we will never be successful in the long term.

Objective Reality

Facts are stubborn things; and whatever may be our wishes,
our inclinations, or the dictates of our passions,
they cannot alter the state of facts and evidence.
—John Adams

When I emphasize *truth*, I mean the objective reality of our lives and existence that we—those of us who are sane and think logically—can all categorically agree with. This includes facts and information that cannot be disputed and are universally true, whether or not someone chooses to acknowledge them. Truth supports and encompasses absolute rules and principles that can be reliably used and continually applied everywhere.

Some examples include: two plus two always equals four, water is necessary to sustain life, gravity exists, in a vacuum light travels at precisely 186,282.397 miles per second, mathematics are necessary to reverse engineer the physical world, companies have to be profitable to survive, financial calculations require knowledge of algebra, and reason allows human beings to think logically and draw inferences.

Subjective Opinions, Wishful Thinking

When you argue with reality, you lose—but
only 100% of the time.
—Byron Katie

Truth does not include subjective opinions about theories, situations, and information that rational and sensible people can disagree with. For example, individuals can argue about how much humidity is tolerable when playing tennis; how the moon was formed; whether the ocean is blue, blue-green, light-blue, or dark-blue in color; how much exercise is needed to stay reasonably fit; what size computer screen is most comfortable to use; and whether a Riesling or a Chardonnay wine should be served with fish.

If we mistake wishful thinking, flawed beliefs, irrational emotions, and unsubstantiated biases for "truth," then we're in trouble. Hoping truth will bend to our misguided desires and incorrect assumptions is catastrophic. Reality will not conform to our subjective wishes. In fact, reality will break us and destroy us if we choose to ignore it.

Jumping out of an airplane without a parachute and wishing that gravity will not work, will result in severe injury and mostly likely death. Ignoring a pathological boss—who has repeatedly lied to us, manipulated us, intimidated us, and unfairly passed us over for promotion—and hoping that he'll become an honest and decent man, will insure that we waste our time working in a dead-end job, endure unnecessary suffering and stress, and sacrifice our life and talents to benefit a shameless bastard who doesn't deserve it. Refusing to listen to the truthful advice of trusted friends and family members to confront a serious obesity problem or an alcohol addiction, will lead to diabetes, liver disease, heart attack, or death.

Truth – Effective Shield and Powerful Tool
Truth is confirmed by inspection and delay;
falsehood by haste and uncertainty.
—Tacitus

Truth is also an effective shield against the growing tsunami of lies and falsehoods assaulting us daily from every direction. Deploy it to protect yourself and your loved ones and avoid treacherous situations. Use it to distance yourself from liars, cheaters, and con artists. Depend on it to guard against unprincipled and pathological individuals at work and in your personal life. Use it to avoid scams, hoaxes, and all sorts of fraudulent schemes. Employ it to help and teach others how to seek and use the truth to protect themselves also.

Truth is the most important and powerful tool you have. It helps you discern the core reality of what is really going on with you and around you. It gives you the ability to see beyond the facade of others. It allows you to notice the inconsistencies and contradictions, to spot the inevitable red flags that indicate falsehood, deception, and danger.

Rely on truth at all times and in every place, in all areas of your life. Speak the truth as often as you can. Use it to evaluate your current workplace, co-workers, and superiors; as well as other individuals in your life, including friends and family members. Use truth to assess your own character, knowledge, experience, and unique skills and abilities. Use it to appraise your current financial and economic situation. Employ truth to increase your knowledge, sharpen your skills, and deepen your wisdom and understanding. Use it to explore potential future opportunities for your personal growth, career advancement, and financial investments.

Use truth to discover hidden value that others have missed. Deploy it to find better resolutions to problems. Use it to devise innovative solutions or explore opportunities that haven't been considered. Use it to find unmet market needs and unique and profitable niches in the marketplace. Rely on it to plan, prepare, and start your own business or organization, or acquire another business that can be improved. Embrace truth to give yourself the best chance to find the freedom and happiness you desire.

Always Seek the Truth

If you look for truth, you may find comfort in the end;
if you look for comfort you will not get either comfort or
truth only soft soap and wishful thinking to begin,
and in the end, despair.
—C.S. Lewis

Always seek the truth. If you have mastered this skill, then everything else can work. If you haven't, then nothing else matters, because it will ultimately lead to ruin. Only the truth can set you free. Truth can pave the way for genuine happiness and authentic success to arrive, nothing else can. All roads that lead away from the truth, will destroy and enslave you, every single time. That's an absolute reality of life. Ignore it at your own peril.

When we become constant truth seekers, we reap considerable and powerful long-term benefits. Truth allows us to see everything around us clearly, so we can determine what to do, how to do it, and when to do it. Truth helps us answer the fundamental questions of who we are and why we were created. Truth enables us to understand the implications of our actions and accurately predict the future consequences of our choices. Without truth as a foundational and permanent element in our lives we cannot be truly free, happy, or successful in a lasting and meaningful way. (For a refresher on the meaning of freedom, happiness, and success, please see Chapter 3.)

Apply and Remember

- Always live in reality; be a hardcore realist.

- Don't allow flawed thinking to twist the truth.

- Don't allow your emotions or biases to obscure reality.

- Seek to discern and discover the truth in all things and all areas of your life.

- Be honest with yourself; see yourself as you really are.

- Don't allow your ego to distort how you perceive reality and the truth.

- Objectively evaluate your character, experience, knowledge, unique skills, and abilities.

- Don't believe everything you hear, see, or read.

- Test and verify all advice you're given, and all theories and ideas you discover, to determine how truthful and accurate they are.

- Speak the truth as often as you can.

- Be careful of organizations where truth is scarce or truth speakers are silenced or persecuted.

- Don't confide in or trust anyone who doesn't speak the truth, or lies habitually.

- Stay away from those who constantly twist the truth.

- Don't associate with those who are afraid of the truth or hate the truth.

- Make friends with those who speak the truth, both at work and in your personal life.

- Teach, encourage, and help others to live in reality and seek the truth; if they're willing and ready to listen.

CHAPTER 9

Yes, Things Really are That Bad

We have over 130 million people in our workforce who go home every day, feeling they work for a company that doesn't care about them. That is seven out of eight people in the workforce. These are our mothers, our fathers, our brothers, our sisters, our sons, and our daughters.
—Bob Chapman

At this point, some of you may be wondering whether I'm blowing things out of proportion. "Are there really that many dysfunctional companies and toxic organizations out there? Are there tens of millions of employees who are discouraged and disillusioned with their jobs and superiors? Are there that many people who hate their jobs and despise their managers? Are things really that bad? Maybe the warnings and exhortations in previous chapters were just creative license by the author to generate attention. Maybe the alarming tone is meant to create a sense of urgency in order to sell more books."

No, I'm not making this up. Yes, things really are that bad. I'm not exaggerating the seriousness of the problems. This leadership disaster is real and on-going. This workplace human tragedy has lasted for decades. It's not just my experience. This is what millions of others also encounter at work every single day.

Solid Evidence: Gallup Q12 Employee Engagement Surveys

The most powerful and accurate evidence of this leadership and human crisis comes from the Gallup organization, a US-based analytics and consulting company. Starting in the 1990s, Gallup developed its "Q12 survey," a set of 12 questions that it uses to measure employee engagement in companies and organizations in the United States and around the world.

Gallup analysts base their findings on data collected from "more than 195,600 U.S. employees, more than 31 million respondents, and insight from advising leading Fortune 1000 companies." Across nearly two decades, Gallup surveys consistently show that approximately 30% of employees in the United States are actively "engaged" at work. This reached a low of 26% in 2000 and peaked to 34% in 2018. On average, 17% of American workers are "actively disengaged." This has fluctuated from a high of 20% in 2007–2008, to a low of 13% in 2018. The remaining 53% of people working in U.S. companies are "not engaged."

Engaged, Not Engaged, Actively Disengaged

Gallup has created three main engagement categories to group employees. Based on how individuals answer the 12 questions in Gallup's Q12 survey, they're classified as either: (1) Engaged, (2) Not Engaged, or (3) Actively Disengaged. Here's how Gallup defines each of these categories, from the company's *State of the American Workplace* report:

(1) Engaged Employees = 30%

"Engaged employees work with passion and feel a profound connection to their company. They drive innovation and move the organization forward."

(2) Not Engaged Employees = 53%

"Not Engaged employees are essentially 'checked out.' They're sleepwalking through their workday, putting time—but no energy or passion—into their work."

(3) Actively Disengaged Employees = 17%

"Actively Disengaged employees aren't just unhappy at work; they're busy acting out their unhappiness. Each day, these workers undermine what their engaged coworkers accomplish."

Approximately 70% of American Workers Are Not Actively Engaged

It's sad, really, how a negative workplace can impact our lives and the way we feel about ourselves. The situation is reaching pandemic heights—most people go to work at jobs they dislike, supervised by people who don't care about them, and directed by senior leaders who are often clueless about where to take the company.
—Leigh Branham and Mark Hirschfeld

The comprehensive multi-year Gallup surveys confirm that, on average, only 30% of employees in the American economy are performing at or near their full capacity and potential. These are the most passionate, productive, and innovative individuals across organizations. They're the best employees, the most valuable resources. They're the ones primarily responsible for the profitability, growth, and success of most companies.

Does this mean that the other 70% of employees, who are not engaged or actively disengaged, are just terrible employees? So many human beings simply lack motivation, passion, and initiative? Tens of millions have no desire to contribute, work hard, and give their best? A staggering 70% of American workers are lazy, show up only to collect a paycheck, hate their jobs, or want to create havoc at work for no reason whatsoever? Is it possible that 70% of all employees in the United States have "checked out" by chance?

Of course not! It's not the employees, it's the leadership. These human beings behave this way because of incompetent, unprincipled, and sociopathic superiors who mismanage and mistreat them at all organizational levels. These employees are actively being demotivated and abused by managers and executives who fail to practice even the most basic leadership principles necessary to properly lead others. Many in charge do the exact opposite of what they're supposed to be doing. No wonder millions of American workers have stopped caring or have given up.

Confirmation From Experience

My own experiences as an employee, manager, executive, consultant, and university professor—spanning more than 34 years across multiple companies and organizations—reflect the same dreadful reality. Additionally, in discussing and analyzing these management and leadership issues with thousands of graduate and undergraduate students in the last two decades, a vast majority of them confirmed what the Gallup surveys indicate. Good leadership and healthy organizations were overwhelmingly the exception, rather than the rule. It didn't matter if someone worked in a small or medium-size business, large company, billion dollar corporation, government agency, non-profit, or university. Whether it was interns, employees, supervisors, managers, directors, executives, or business owners, they all shared similar experiences with awful bosses and dysfunctional workplace environments.

Why a Revolution is Needed

The lack of effective, ethical, and principled human-centered and value-driven leadership is a fundamental flaw at the core of many companies and organizations. This is why I wrote that a revolution is needed to fight against it. Small measures just won't do. Individually, we lack the power and resources required to change these dysfunctional behemoths. Our best option is to dig our tunnel and escape; then seek better opportunities in healthier companies or start our own business and build it right from the ground up. Both alternatives require a long-term focus, lots of preparation and planning, hard work, and discipline. So what are you waiting for? Start today!

Apply and Remember

- On average, only 30% of U.S. employees are engaged, while 70% are not engaged or actively disengaged. This had remained consistent for almost two decades.

- If you happen to be one of the 30% who are engaged and your company treats you well, then consider yourself fortunate and be thankful for your job. You can pursue your freedom and happiness, while continuing to work for your current organization.

- If you are in the 70% group who are not engaged and it's due to a poor or dysfunctional work situation, then you should start looking for opportunities elsewhere and plan your eventual exit. There's little chance you'll find freedom or happiness working for that organization.

CHAPTER 10

Disposable Employees, Discarded Lives

*We're destroying people and killing our culture because
we send people home after treating them as objects and
functions, instead of caring about them as human beings.*
—Bob Chapman

For years, across most companies, corporations, and organizations, one consistent message has been sent to employees: "You are disposable." Management's behavior communicates to employees the following: "We don't care about your life or your family. We own you. Everyone is replaceable. We can and will fire you at any time for any reason. You're on your own."

Such reprehensible attitudes reflect how superiors deal with the human beings who spend most of their waking hours working in their organizations. They use fear as a weapon to intimidate and control their employees. They deploy fear to silence individuals, to force them to comply and accept their fate. "Be lucky you have a job," is used to threaten anyone who questions anything that management does, regardless of how incompetent, reckless, unfair, destructive, or downright stupid it is. They act like feudal lords or tyrants, and treat us like serfs or indentured servants, not free men and women.

This is the same loud message I received as an employee of different companies and universities for more than three decades. Likewise, thousands of students I've helped over the years shared similar experiences with managers and executives in their workplaces. Rarely did these students encounter businesses or institutions that truly cared about them, their families, or their lives. They were treated as a number, a gear in the machinery; an object to be used, exploited, and discarded at will.

If you work for an organization where you are considered disposable and management treats you as an easily replaceable part, then you should begin to consider other options. You need to realistically determine the risks and dangers of continuing to invest more time, energy, and effort into a career that can be instantly terminated for any reason. Do you really want to gamble with your future knowing that your superiors can fire you at any time, no matter how valuable, productive, and loyal you are? This chapter will cover multiple examples and warnings for you to take into account when evaluating your current work circumstances and contemplating better long-term alternatives.

Inhuman University

It's unclear just where exactly these executives learned to be so heartless and cruel. I don't recall seeing these particular anti-human management approaches listed in any books or textbooks on management and leadership. Maybe they got MBAs in Anti-Management or Pseudo-Leadership from Inhuman University. Or maybe they apprenticed as Mafia enforcers to hone their people skills. I hear some folks will do anything to make money and get power; maybe these are some of them. It's quite possible the phrase "would throw their own grandmother under a bus" was created upon encountering such specimens.

Don't get me wrong. I'm not claiming that all companies and organizations take this stance. I'm not saying all managers behave this way. There are good companies, decent business owners, and competent bosses and executives who conduct themselves in an exemplary manner and treat employees well. Unfortunately, they are the exceptions, not the norm. As the Gallup data confirms, only 30% of U.S. employees are fortunate enough to work for organizations that care about them and treat them decently. The other 70% have most likely been given the "you're disposable and easily replaceable" treatment at some point in their careers.

Human Tragedy Becoming the New Normal

Employers have gone away from the idea that an employee is a long-term asset to the company, someone to be nurtured and developed, to a new notion that they are disposable.
—Barbara Ehrenreich

This human tragedy has become the "new normal" in organizations. If you haven't experienced it or heard about it from a friend or relative, you may have seen or read news stories describing the despicable manner in which companies treat and dispose of employees.

Here's a sampling of the stories I've come across, read about, and heard directly from students in my university courses:

- An entire department is taken to lunch by its manager. After enjoying a nice meal, the group returns to work.

Waiting outside their building are several HR representatives holding boxes full of their personal belongings. They've all just been unceremoniously fired. Security officers are there to prevent the employees from entering the building. They are not allowed get back to their cubicles or say their goodbyes. Interestingly enough, their manager had vanished a few minutes after lunch, claiming a family emergency had occurred. He wasn't let go, of course.

- An experienced director is recruited to participate in a re-engineering project lasting 18 months. He will have to step away from his current role, but the executive in charge promises that the director's job will be secure upon project completion. The director leaves his position and joins the re-engineering team. He dutifully performs his responsibilities and assists the corporation for the duration of the initiative. Once the project is completed, the director is immediately fired, by the same executive who "guaranteed" that the position was going to be "safe."

- Employees at an e-commerce company are asked to attend a staff meeting. The high-level executive explains that the venture encountered financial difficulties and layoffs are necessary. He tells the employees to check their emails to find out who's being fired by the end of the day. The executive then rushes out of the room before anyone can ask any questions.

- Employee is notified that her organization is closing its offices in the city where she works. To keep her job she is offered the option to relocate to another location, across the country. Employee sells her home and moves to the new city with her husband and children. A couple of months after starting work in her new office she is laid off. She is given no explanation, no warning, no apology.

- A manager with a solid track record, a loyal and hard-working long-time employee, is asked by his boss to train two new employees. The executive tells the manager these individuals are the additional resources the manager had previously requested to assist him with increased workloads. Part of the training requires the manager to transfer his expertise to the new employees so they learn everything he knows and does. The manager is grateful that he finally obtained the help he needed; he won't have to work constant overtime. anymore.

  Six months later the manager gets a bonus and commendation from his boss, for a job "well done" onboarding the new employees. Three months after that, he's fired and escorted out of his office by security. Manager later discovers he was "costing" the company too much money. His boss had no intention of helping him. The executive wanted two people on staff for the price of one. The bonus and commendation were meant to fool the manager and preclude him from becoming suspicious; give him a false sense of security and allow the new employees more time to absorb critical information and report back to the shameless executive.

Even among businesses that are still operating, you see numerous companies with a proud heritage that are trying to shrink their way to success, routinely announcing mass layoffs and never-ending "restructurings" in desperate bids

to survive. You see people losing their livelihoods, but also their sense of self-worth and hope for the future.
—Bob Chapman

Homestore.com – Fraudsters Conducted Demeaning Layoffs

I formerly worked as director of web development at Homestore.com (rebranded to Move.com now). Homestore operated the Realtor.com website, the largest real estate listings website at the time (during 1999–2002). Homestore's management team was unable to capitalize on the unique position and strategic advantages the company had in the marketplace, and squandered the resources and talent they were entrusted with. Facing significant losses (due to their own incompetence and unethical behavior) and with no effective leadership and strategic management solutions from executives, Homestore decided to cut costs via multiple waves of layoffs.

Here's how Homestore executives handled the firing of employees:

1. Do not disclose anything to your employees in advance and do not communicate your intentions or reasons for doing anything.

2. Reassure employees that their jobs are secure, that the company is doing great, and that layoff rumors are false. Lie to their face: "You have nothing to worry about," the week before the imminent layoffs.

3. In order to manipulate and intimidate employees who are hoping for advancement or a promised raise, hint in pri-

vate that layoffs could be coming and threaten them with the statement: "Be lucky you still have a job!"

4. Keep the entire organization guessing until the very last moment; typically the morning of the layoffs. On the designated day, start calling each employee one by one into the executive's office and close the door. Give them "we care about you" speech, make them sign a waiver, and withhold their last paycheck until they release the company of all liability. Repeat this process for hours on end, until every employee is let go.

5. Escort employees back to their offices or cubicles and give them until the end of the day to clear out everything and say their goodbyes. If they're especially talented or essential employees, have security watch over the process to insure these individuals don't suddenly turn into criminals, after years of loyal service.

6. Have the CEO publicly blame the firings on the economy and declare that he felt "bad about the layoffs," but insist they were necessary. Have the same CEO send emails to the entire organization telling everyone how "incredibly proud" he was of how his "team has met our many challenges," bemoaning how this was "the single most difficult day in" his professional life, and boasting how the layoffs will "maintain the health of the business."(These statements turned out to be incredibly ironic given this CEO's contemporaneous criminal conduct which lead to the financial collapse of the company; mentioned below.)

7. A few days later, ask employees who survived the firing to write individual reports to justify why their positions

should exist, describe what they are working on, and explain the benefits they bring to Homestore; in other words, "tell us why we shouldn't fire you next."

8. Finally, issue harsh private warnings to remaining managers that absolute loyalty is expected; they are not allowed to question or challenge what executives are doing. Threaten them with immediate firing if they speculate about the company condition or discuss current or future layoffs with anyone. Remind them how fortunate they are to still work there.

Interestingly enough, many of the executives responsible for these layoffs were later found guilty of financial, accounting, and securities fraud. They faked tens of millions of dollars of non-existent revenues (via "round-trip barter transactions") to illegally inflate reported corporate income and deceive stockholders and investors. Meanwhile these same executives, including the CEO, exercised their stock options and raked in millions of dollars of ill-gotten gains. These con artists were not only abusing and mistreating their employees, but they were defrauding shareholders and investors as well.

Thankfully justice prevailed. To date, eleven Homestore executives have been convicted or have plead guilty to multiple security violations and other federal criminal charges stemming from their involvement in the extensive fraud scheme. In 2006, Stuart Wolff, former Homestore CEO (same one who sent those deceptive emails to employees), was found guilty of 18 counts of "conspiracy, insider trading, making false regulatory filings and lying to auditors" and sentenced to 15 years in federal prison. According to the FBI, other Homestore executives were also convicted and have "received sentences ranging from probation to 27 months in custody," in addition to having to pay back millions of dollars of fraudulently obtained funds from exercising their stock options. (In 2010 Wolff's sentence was reduced on appeal to four and a half years of jail time.) Federal prosecutors estimate that Homestore investors lost approximately $1.6 billion after the fraud was discovered.

Disney IT – The Unhappiest Place on Earth

But even Homestore doesn't match Disney in sheer callousness and cruelty when laying off employees. The executives of The Walt Disney Company, of "The Happiest Place on Earth" fame, win the prize in utter ruthlessness and inhumanity when firing their own "Cast Members," as the company refers to its employees. Management not only destroyed these individuals' careers and disposed of them in an arbitrary manner, but they also repeatedly insulted and humiliated them during the whole process.

Starting in late 2014 into early 2015, Disney fired approximately 250 Information Technology (IT) employees and outsourced their jobs to cheaper foreign workers brought into the United States by outsourcing companies exploiting federal H-1B visa loopholes (which Congress still hasn't fixed). The layoffs started just ten days after Disney's CEO Bob Iger had announced that the company's quarterly earnings were up over 20 percent. This followed a sustained record of healthy financial results for the corporation.

The discarded individuals were some of the best and most experienced IT employees at Disney. They were particularly knowledgeable and hard working. They were doing excellent work for the company. They were highly regarded by co-workers and managers. Many had repeatedly been recognized by management for their superior efforts. Several had earned the distinguished Disney "blue badge" which indicated they were "Partners in Excellence" and had consistently gone above and beyond in helping their peers.

One of the fired Disney IT engineers, a ten-year veteran with an excellent reputation and solid track record, described the infamous and wicked process that management used to dispose of human beings and what happened to him and dozens of others:

1. Employees were called to an unexpected early morning meeting with a Disney executive. No advanced warning or information was provided to anyone.

2. At that meeting, the executive announced that everyone in the room would lose their jobs within the next 90 days. Their current jobs were being transferred to foreign workers which the Disney employees would be forced to train. If they did not cooperate fully with management's demands, they would not receive their severance pay. The employees where also warned not to discuss the meeting with anyone else in the company.

3. The sudden news was devastating and demoralizing to the Disney employees. As related by the fired IT engineer, some employees in the meeting "had tears streaming down their faces, others had completely broken down and were crying out loud and one was murmuring 'no, this can't be' as they were marched out of the room."

4. During the first 30 days the foreign H-1B visa workers began learning and capturing all job information from the Disney workers. IT employees attended daily mandatory

"Knowledge Transfer" sessions and stared training their replacements. All sessions were recorded and documented. Disney employees then had to review and validate the recordings.

5. During the next 30 days, the replacements worked side by side with Disney employees. The humiliation continued as the less experienced foreign workers assumed all job responsibilities while the existing employees were forced to continually help and answer their questions.

6. In the final 30 days, the shameful, demeaning, and demoralizing transition reached its peak. Disney IT employees watched helplessly as their foreign replacements completely took over their jobs. "The last day we turned in our mobile phones, laptops, ID badges along with our dignity and we were ushered out the door as temporary foreign workers took over our jobs," writes the same fired IT engineer.

Disney: No Remorse, No Apologies, No Regrets

Even after this travesty was publicly exposed, Disney did not apologize or admit that it did anything wrong in how it handled the degrading layoffs. Neither Disney nor any of its representatives have showed any remorse or expressed regret for the abhorrent manner in which corporate executives disposed of several hundred American employees to make way for cheaper foreign workers. Disney executives were also not ashamed of abusing the H-1B visa process (which was not created to help corporations replace its American workers with low-cost foreign substitutes) to get rid of its highly experienced and qualified IT employees, thus violating the spirit and intent of the H-1B foreign visa program.

No Guaranteed Jobs, Decency Still Needed

I'm not saying that all individuals are entitled to lifetime employment. No one "deserves" a job. There are no guaranteed positions. Technically all of us are "replaceable." That's life. That's reality. Companies and organizations need to continue to operate and do business. They need to replace employees that fail to perform effectively or violate company policies. Management can hire and fire anyone they choose, as long as they do it fairly, ethically, lawfully, and decently.

However, telling employees that "everyone is replaceable," is the most unkind thing to say to them. Constantly reminding people that "they can be fired at any time" is abusive. Threatening them with the loss of their jobs to keep them in line is both insulting and degrading. It's informing them that they're worthless as far as management is concerned. It robs them of their dignity. It crushes their spirit. It's inhuman. Yet, that's precisely what passes for "management" in far too many instances. Any wonder why I wrote that a revolution is necessary?

How to Protect Yourself

- Pay close attention to how executives view the people in your organization. Listen to the language used and the messages that management sends out. Do they consider human beings valuable resources? Do they care for employees as unique and precious individuals? Or do they treat employees as disposable or interchangeable parts of a machine?

- Observe executives' attitude and behavior towards subordinates. This will indicate exactly what they think about employees. Are they truthful, generous, compassionate, caring, understanding, and kind, in word and deed? Or are they deceiving, stingy, selfish, arrogant, condescending, insulting, or abusive, in speech and conduct?

- Watch carefully what superiors actually do and you will get a better sense and understanding of their actual beliefs. Notice how superiors handle employees in good and bad times, and in emergency situations. The real character of a person shows through in times of crisis.

- When the organization encounters financial difficulties does it immediately start getting rid of employees? Does it consider people as just another "expense" to be cut back quickly? Does management use outsourcing as a "solution" to every problem? Are highly paid employees often fired first, regardless of how experienced, loyal, and productive they are?

- Pay attention to how the company handles the process of laying off employees. Is it similar to any of the scenarios covered in this chapter? Do you notice any of the same warning signs? If this is how they treat others, this is how they'll deal with you also.

- There is no safety or security working for any organization that believes in throwaway employees and regards human beings as no different than any other asset like furniture, machinery, or computer equipment. Even if you are loyal, do an excellent job, and consistently deliver value, your job may still be eliminated indiscriminately.

It's not worth risking your future by working for an untrustworthy organization.

- Use the additional guidance, advice, and recommendations provided in this book to help you determine the right approach and direction to follow to defend yourself, protect your current job, find a better position, or consider starting your own business.

CHAPTER 11

How Organizations Demotivate Employees

*A bad manager can take a good staff and destroy it,
causing the best employees to flee and
the remainder to lose all motivation.*

—author unknown

Even when employees aren't treated as disposable, organizations still find a myriad of other ways to demotivate them, demoralize them, and negatively affect their productivity. Listed below are many unethical, dysfunctional, abusive, and destructive management attitudes and practices that I have personally experienced as an employee or witnessed while consulting for various companies, corporations, universities, and non-profit institutions. Each of these will corrode organizational cohesiveness, alienate employees, foment suspicion, fuel resentment, and increase cynicism. All of these misbehaviors will lead employees to lose respect for their superiors and lose trust in their organization. Collectively these dysfunctional approaches will destroy an organization from the inside and transform it into a private hell for the good and decent employees still working there.

How to Demotivate Employees
Dysfunctional Management Playbook

1. Talk down to employees and make them feel powerless and insignificant.

2. Repeatedly lie to them and mangle the truth, and then pretend that you didn't; blame them for "misunderstanding" or "misremembering" when they point out various inconsistencies or lies.

3. Constantly remind employees—in an arrogant or condescending tone—how fortunate they are to be working for you.

4. Don't listen to what employees have to say.

5. Pretend to listen to what they say, then disregard it.

6. Ignore employees' suggestions, innovative ideas, and constructive feedback, even when they can improve the company's product(s) or service(s), enhance customer service, optimize processes, reduce costs, or increase profitability.

7. Ask employees for feedback on what's going on with the organization, what problems need to be corrected, and what positive changes should be made, then promptly ignore everything they recommend.

8. Send out multiple emails, newsletters, and other internal company communications telling employees how much management cares about them and how important they are to the company, then continually act in ways that contradict everything written and claimed.

9. Don't give employees any real autonomy or freedom to fix problems, make improvements, or find innovative solutions.

10. Micromanage their work and constantly override or reverse their legitimate decisions and practical recommendations.

11. Drown them in overbearing processes and bureaucratic procedures that give more power and control to managers, but create useless busy work for employees while contributing nothing to employee productivity or helping them complete work more efficiently and productively.

12. Don't recognize or reward superior work or key employees' accomplishments.

13. Take credit for the employees' important accomplishments and successes, but blame them for all missteps or mistakes, even when they're not at fault.

14. Make promises you know you can't keep or offer them opportunities that will never materialize.

15. Create a rigid multi-layered bureaucratic management hierarchy and pecking order based solely on status and power, and make it virtually impossible for front-line employees or managers to reach or communicate substantively with senior managers and executives.

16. Pay employees differently for doing the same functional work or delivering similar productivity.

17. Increase workloads and job responsibilities for some employees, while pretending they won't be doing more work and getting paid the same.

18. Practice unjustified favoritism and treat employees capriciously.

19. Hire the wrong individuals based on subjective criteria and without regard of the needs and concerns of current employees.

20. Promote the wrong people based on what's best for you or other executives, not for the team, department, or company as a whole.

21. Purposely pass people over for promotion to "show them who's boss, keep them in line, or teach them a lesson."

22. Reward and promote only those employees who always agree with you and constantly suck up to you, regardless of how mediocre or unqualified they are or how poorly they fit in with their teams and departments.

23. Offer pay raises or cost-of-living increases to some employees, while ignoring others who do the same work and contribute just as much to company profitability; pretend this is not happening and silence (or fire) anyone who questions the unfairness.

24. Don't give long-term, productive, and loyal employees any stake in the business.

25. Pay them fixed salaries and require unlimited hours of work, even on the weekends.

26. Don't provide profit-sharing or other performance-based or merit-based rewards to employees, while giving them to directors and executives.

27. Thank employees for showing great initiative and delivering excellence or superior achievements (above and beyond their normal job responsibilities), but don't give

them any meaningful or valuable reward beyond the "thank you" email, card, plaque, cake, balloons, or a minimal value gift card.

28. Demand that employees sacrifice (lose benefits, take a pay cut, and/or work more for less pay) "for the good of the organization," while executives pay, benefits, and bonuses stay the same or even rise (during or after the crisis has passed).

29. Increase senior executives compensation even when the company's overall performance, profitability, or long-term competitive position are negatively impacted by the executives' mismanagement or incompetence.

30. Use a company's poor performance, lower stock price, stagnating sales, and/or decreasing revenues or profitability, as an excuse and reason why employees won't get raises or bonuses in a particular year, while senior managers and executives still get raises, bonuses, profit sharing, or stock options in that same year.

31. Don't reassure employees in times of uncertainty, change, or crises. As a matter of fact, act in ways that makes them even more anxious, suspicious, and fearful.

32. Keep them in the dark about key organizational problems, financial difficulties, or upcoming layoffs.

33. Punish all employees for the abuses or mistakes of a few; then change policies and procedures to further burden and penalize everyone, including those individuals who did nothing wrong.

34. Promote a win-lose confrontational culture where employees are encouraged to achieve success and monetary gains at the expense of others who work there.

35. Allow constant departmental in-fighting that destabilizes organizational cohesiveness and centralizes power in senior executives only (better known as "divide and conquer").

36. Remind employees that they're disposable and insure that management conduct persistently corroborates this mentality.

37. Confirm that anyone can be easily replaced by making examples of a few individuals on a regular basis.

38. Make employees operate in perpetual uncertainty and in constant fear of losing their jobs.

39. Threaten employees with "be lucky you have a job" when they speak truthfully about serious organizational issues, challenge incompetent managers, or stand up to abusive superiors.

40. When employees try to resolve unfair or unjust organizational situations, shrug your shoulders and tell them: "No one is forcing you to stay" or "You can always quit."

The best don't stick around when you treat them poorly,
only the desperate do.
— Shannon L. Alder

Once multiple instances of the aforementioned dysfunctional behaviors become normalized and start to spread across an organization, then employee dissatisfaction and disengagement will increase. The workplace culture will degrade. Pessimism will grow. Trust will erode. Productivity and innovation will decline. Quality of work will be negatively impacted. Great employees will begin to leave. Then the good ones will quit. The remaining employees will stop caring, stop speaking out, and stop trying to address problems or improve anything inside the company. They will "go to gray." They will do the minimal work required of them and nothing more.

Concurrently, the wrong people will benefit and prosper. The worst people will stay in their management positions. The mediocre and the incompetent will keep their jobs. The cheerleaders of this dysfunction will be promoted. The tacit enablers of the status quo will be rewarded for their indifference and silence. Sociopaths will thrive (see Chapters 18 and 19) and reach the highest levels of leadership in the organization. The inmates will firmly be in charge of the asylum.

If this pathology persists over longer periods of time, a human resources crisis will envelop the entire company. Disaster (financial, ethical, legal, criminal, etc.) will inevitably follow. No one will be spared as the organization eventually collapses.

These attitudes and approaches are the exact opposites of how genuine leaders should ethically, justly, fairly, and capitalistically treat their employees. These behaviors make a mockery out of the universally true principle that an organization's employees are its most valuable resources (see Chapter 14).

None of these practices are taught in any business, management, leadership, or other academic course or program, as an ethical and effective way to lead and manage others. None of these practices have ever been proven to motivate employees, boost their morale, or increase their loyalty, trust, or productivity. They don't help a company achieve long-term success or sustained profitability. Yet, managers and executives continue to adopt these anti-human strategies to "get results, get the job done, or make their numbers." Demoralizing employees and insuring the long-term failure of the company are the only things management ultimately accomplishes.

EXERCISE

Measure Dysfunction in Your Organization

Review the 40 dysfunctional scenarios presented above. Have you experienced or witnessed any of these situations at work? Are any of those attitudes analogous to how managers or executives behave in your organization? Count how many of the examples listed match or come close to what you've seen or experienced in your current workplace. Then compare the total with the keys below.

Great organization (0-1) – If you've encountered none or only one of the 40 bad practices (and it's not one of the more extreme ones), then you work for a great company. You are one of those fortunate employees who has found a job in a phenomenal organization lead by great leaders. You work for a healthy company. You're probably surrounded by good people and managers. If you like what you do, are paid fairly, and you have opportunities for growth and advancement, then hold on to your job. There's no reason to leave. If the organization stays the course, you will have a promising future there.

Good organization (2-4) – If you have come across two, three, or four of the unfortunate situations (and they're not the more outrageous ones), then you work for a good company. No organization is perfect; even good ones can experience periods of dysfunction. As with the "great" category above, you should hold on to your job, especially if you like what you're working on, are paid decently, and there are growth opportunities. If things improve and some of the bad practices cease, then you may find yourself working for a great company; you'll be rewarded for your patience and endurance. However, if the situation worsens and more dysfunctional practices begin to appear, then you should be more attentive to what's going on and determine why things are changing. See if you can help the organization get back on track. If you don't have enough influence or management ignores your recommendations, then start to consider alternate plans for your career, things may not improve after all.

Average organization (5-9) – If you've seen or encountered five to nine different bad practices, then you work for an average company. This is probably the range in which many organizations operate; not too bad and not too good either, sort of mediocre. Keep a careful watch. If the poor behaviors decrease in number, that means things are improving; your company may be turning into a good organization. If the dysfunction grows, then the organization is heading into serious trouble; you should start exploring the alternatives you considered previously and begin to dig your tunnel in case things worsen and you need to escape.

Dysfunctional organization (10-15) – Once a company experiences more than 10 of these dysfunctional situations, a tipping point has been crossed. The likelihood that things will get better decreases significantly. Continue to dig your tunnel, save more money, reduce your overhead expenses, explore other income-earning opportunities, and actively begin to look for a different job.

Highly dysfunctional organization (16-20) – If you've noticed more than 16 dysfunctional scenarios, the decay has become institutionalized. There is little chance things will improve. They'll probably get much worse. Accelerate the digging of your tunnel. Increase your networking and speed up your job search efforts. Prepare to exit, there's no future with such an organization. In a relatively short time this will become a toxic company.

Toxic organization (21-30) – At this level dysfunction is rampant. There is no chance that things will get better (unless the company is acquired by another healthy organization and all current dysfunctional managers and sociopathic executives are fired). Use your tunnel to escape the toxic work environment that surrounds you. Leave as soon as you are able. Staying is hazardous to your physical, mental, and spiritual health. Hopefully, the early warnings and months of planning and preparation will help you depart without endangering your financial situation and allow you to find a better job or pursue your entrepreneurial aspirations.

Hellish organization (31+) – Past 31 different bad practices, the dysfunction has fully metastasized and will rapidly lead to collapse. Get out now! Do not look back! It's not worth losing your sanity over a paycheck. Any other job will be better than having to work in such a horrific organization.

Note: This exercise is not scientific. The 40 different demotivational situations presented are not created equal. Some are much more serious and destructive than others. Therefore, when counting how many exist in your organization be cognizant of that fact and adjust your evaluation accordingly.

CHAPTER 12

Dysfunctional Companies Ignore Reality

I reject your reality, and substitute my own.
—Adam Savage

A common characteristic of all dysfunctional organizations is the systematic abandonment and eventual suppression of the truth, and its substitution with half-truths, distortions, and lies. Once truth no longer supports and validates everything that happens in a company, management's ability to understand what is really going on, make the right decisions, and take corrective action is compromised. Executives gradually lose touch with their employees and their customers. Poor decision-making becomes rampant. Trust erodes and problems engulf the company. If this decay is not reversed, then the dysfunctional organization degenerates into a toxic workplace. Problem solvers are ignored, truth seekers are discouraged, and truth speakers are silenced. Management inevitably loses touch with reality and pretends things are fine when they're actually getting worse. More disasters inevitably follow as employee morale rapidly declines and employee disengagement spikes.

Denial of reality and avoidance of truth frequently become routine in dysfunctional and toxic organizations, at multiple levels, especially the highest ones where executives congregate. Highly paid, safe in their positions, and secure in their ivory towers, these senior managers could care less about their subordinates below. Executive are too busy looking out for themselves and preoccupied with maximizing their own compensation. They're out of touch with employees. They can't be bothered with the objective reality of what's happening with their organizations, products, services, and customers. They're not interested in how this negatively affects the long-term success of their enterprises and the well-being of the other human beings who work there.

Why is this information relevant to your work situation? Because, as we've covered previously, truth is necessary to help us live in reality. Seeking the truth allows us to discern what's really going on around us and make the right decisions, including in our workplace. This is universally true for everyone, including the managers of your company. If those individuals do not embrace and practice truth, then their judgment and leadership capabilities will be severely impaired. They will be unable to manage and lead effectively. The organization will decline, become dysfunctional, then turn toxic, and ultimately collapse.

You cannot have a fulfilling and happy career in such an environment. There's no safe job and secure future in any company where truth is ignored and falsehoods rule. The sooner you determine whether you work in a dysfunctional or toxic environment, the sooner you can plan your departure and adequately defend yourself in the meantime.

There are several warning signs that truth is becoming extinct in an organization. It's noticeable when executives disregard the growing disconnect between the corporate slogan and the real culture of the company. It's confirmed when top-level managers progressively ignore problem solvers and silence truth speakers.

Disconnect Between Corporate Slogans and Reality

Accuracy of statement is one of the first elements of truth; inaccuracy is a near kin to falsehood.
—Tryon Edwards

An early indicator that a company doesn't value truth is the disconnect between corporate slogans, sometimes called "vision statements," and what's actually happening in the workplace. We have all encountered different versions of these catchy phrases: "The customer comes first," "We value our employees," "We empower individuals to do amazing things," "Our people are our greatest assets," "The success of employees is our top priority," "We do better together," "Excellence honors God," and "Honesty is the best policy."

You see these catchphrases plastered in corporate boardrooms, conference rooms, or break rooms. You see them displayed during executive presentations and bragged about at company-wide events. They are repeated in various meetings, employee training sessions, internal email blasts and newsletters, and sometimes in press releases. They're printed in employee manuals and pamphlets.

And that's as far as these "window dressing" slogans go. They're never put into practice. They're never integrated into the culture and daily activities of the organization. They remain fictional in nature. They're not emulated by supervisors, managers, or directors. None of the lofty visions seem to matter much inside the company, especially when observing the actions and attitudes of senior executives. These catchphrases have little or no impact on a company's day-to-day operations. They're not contemplated when directors and top executives plan strategies, direct tactics, or communicate with employees. They don't influence management policies and processes, especially regarding employee evaluation, compensation, recognition, and promotion.

Executives pretend they care about the company, the customers, and the employees, even though their actions prove they care mostly about themselves and their own salaries. Management pretends that the fictional internal culture they propagandize is genuine and expects employees to go along with the sham. Workers have to pretend the make-believe culture exists and ignore the truth in front of their own eyes. If they disagree or challenge the dishonest organizational precepts, employees will pay a heavy price. The last thing dysfunctional management wants is courageous and ethical employees who constantly think rationally and speak truthfully; and dare (gasp!) to hold their superiors accountable.

Ignore Problem Solvers

All deception in the course of life is indeed nothing else
but a lie reduced to practice, and
falsehood passing from words into things.
—Robert Southey

Ignoring problem solvers is the next sign that truth is not valued in an organization. Problem solvers are those employees who notice problems with a company's products, services, processes, or policies, and proactively attempt to fix them. These individuals genuinely care about their organization and the customers it serves. They want to do the right thing. Thinking that management would want to know about these problems and accept any reasonable solutions, these employees alert their managers and offer their recommendations.

And then, these vigilant employees are ignored. Often they're admonished to "mind their own business" or told that the actual problems are not really "problems." Management does nothing to address the specific issues. Meanwhile the problems persist and get worse.

Persistent employees will follow-up with their superiors. Once more they'll offer practical advice to correct the problems, only to be ignored or rebuffed again. In toxic workplaces, employees will also be punished for repeatedly "bothering" executives with their concerns. Eventually industrious problem solvers will give up and stop alerting management. They will realize that sticking their necks out is not worth it and doing the right thing is detrimental to their jobs. They will stop caring. They will not even attempt to improve anything in their workplace.

Silence Truth Speakers
Truth is not only violated by falsehood;
it may be equally outraged by silence.
—Henri Frederic Amiel

Silencing truth speakers is the final sign that the dysfunctional organization has turned toxic. This is also known as the "Shoot the Messenger" management approach.

Truth speakers are employees who seek and speak the truth. They are typically the most engaged, ethical, and responsible individuals in an organization. They strive to figure out what's really going on in their company and address the issues effectively.

Truth speakers are the first to notice and point out the discrepancies between a company's slogan and their daily work experiences. They perceive that what's happening with the organization doesn't match the narrative executives project, and they alert superiors and other employees. They see the disconnect between managers and employees and try to correct it. They identify problems and attempt to solve them.

But in toxic organizations, truth seekers and speakers are considered threats, not valuable employees. They are not appreciated, recognized, or thanked. They are intimidated, admonished, marginalized, and silenced. Their desire for the truth is dangerous to the status quo because it exposes organizational idiocy, rot, and corruption. Their commitment to the truth jeopardizes the cushy positions and lavish compensations of superiors, by exposing their incompetence and hypocrisy. Speaking out on these issues warns others and challenges the distortions spread by management.

Truth speakers are constant thorns in the sides of dysfunctional managers and executives. Noticing that the "Emperor has no clothes" is bad enough, but daring to say it out loud is deemed much worse; the ultimate crime in a toxic company. Dissent will not be tolerated. If truth speakers refuse to keep their mouths shut they will be punished and ultimately fired.

EXERCISE

Evaluate if Truth is Important in Your Organization

Good leadership is not just about creating a vision,
but also about creating a culture where
people speak the truth and face the honest facts.
—Jim Collins

Review the questions below to help you evaluate whether truth is important in your organization and truth speakers are tolerated and appreciated. Count how many "Yes" answers you have given and compare with the provided evaluation key to determine whether you work for a healthy, somewhat healthy, average, dysfunctional, or toxic organization. Consider the advice given to either recognize and appreciate healthy companies, or to protect yourself and eventually escape toxic workplaces.

1. Does your company slogan match the workplace culture and reality you experience daily?

2. Do managers and executives emulate the principles and ideals embodied in the company slogan?

3. Do organizational procedures, processes, policies, and initiatives support the organization's slogan?

4. Do you think accountability and transparency are valued across the company?

5. Are accountability and transparency evident in most employees' and management's conduct?

6. Does your immediate manager speak truthfully?

7. Do other managers speak the truth?

8. Do executives deal truthfully with customers, employees, and managers?

9. Are you allowed to speak the truth?

10. Can you disagree with or challenge managers or executives and not be reprimanded?

11. Are other employees able to speak truthfully to superiors without being silenced or chastised?

12. Do you feel comfortable pointing out problems in your organization?

13. Are you allowed to suggest solutions to problems?

14. Can you recommend improvements to products, services, processes, or policies?

15. Do you have freedom to innovate?

16. Has management been receptive to your solutions or improvement ideas?

17. Were any of your solutions or improvement suggestions implemented, either fully or partially?

18. Has management appreciated your efforts in addressing and correcting problems?

19. Were you recognized for successfully correcting problems or making things better?

20. Have you been thanked or rewarded for suggesting needed improvements?

21. Do managers apologize when they are wrong, make mistakes, or behave dishonestly?

22. Do managers acknowledge their own mistakes and take responsibility for their actions?

23. Do managers hold themselves accountable when they violate company policies by applying the required disciplinary consequences to themselves?

24. Do executives apologize when they are wrong or speak untruthfully?

25. Do executives admit their own mistakes and take responsibility for their actions?

26. Do executives hold themselves accountable when they violate company policies by applying the required disciplinary consequences to themselves?

Evaluation Key and Advice

24-26 Yes answers – You work for a **healthy** organization. Truth is valued and treasured across the company. Leaders support a climate where truth matters and is constantly heard. Employees have the freedom to speak and act truthfully. Men and women of character and integrity have nothing to fear from management. Employees are appreciated and recognized for doing the right things. Keep speaking the truth and helping the organization in whatever capacity you can. This is a great place to work and thrive.

20-23 Yes answers – You work for a **moderately healthy** organization. Truth seems mostly valued in your organization. Individuals still have sufficient autonomy to speak out, fix problems, and innovate, but there are some signs that management is drifting away from truth. Keep a careful watch on how truth seekers and truth speakers are treated.

Notice if they still have the ability and opportunity to speak freely. See if they are rewarded and promoted for fixing problems and suggesting real improvements, even when they disagree with management. If the culture improves, you'll be in a better position for future success in your company. If things degrade, then you'll need to take proactive steps to protect yourself and start digging your tunnel.

15-19 Yes answers – You work for an **average** organization. There are many warning signs that truth is no longer a priority in your workplace. Management is moving away from reality. Dysfunction may soon become normalized unless executives reverse course and take concrete steps to confront facts and place truth at the center of all decision-making. Be vigilant. Thoroughly evaluate what's going on. Assess the reactions and attitudes of your co-workers and superiors when truth is spoken. Observe which co-workers and superiors value truth and can be trusted; speak frankly only with them. Don't share your opinions or suggestions with anyone who is untrustworthy or duplicitous. Think about when you should speak and what you say. Choose your battles wisely. Don't stick out your neck for minor or inconsequential issues. Unless your job is threatened or you need to defend yourself, don't challenge or contradict superiors who don't like to hear the truth; and if you have to, be careful what you say and how you say it. Get busy digging your tunnel so you're prepared to leave if things get worse.

9-14 Yes answers – You work for a **dysfunctional** organization. You should make yourself as unnoticeable (invisible) as possible. Remain silent and do not offer solutions to problems, unless death or bodily injury is imminent to others. If innocence is in danger, you must speak out and act to prevent harm. In dysfunctional workplaces everything can and will be used against you. Be prepared to be fired or demoted for speaking the truth to superiors who don't like hearing it. Start looking for another job in earnest. Consider alternative ways to earn a living (consult, start a business, change careers, etc.). Speed up your tunnel digging. Intensify your networking and job search activities. Make every effort to leave before the organization turns toxic.

0-8 Yes answers – You work for a **toxic** organization. Truth no longer matters in your workplace. Management has lost touch with reality. The organization's death spiral will accelerate. There's no hope this company will improve. Working in such an unhealthy environment is harmful to your mental, physical, and spiritual well-being. Leave as soon as possible.

CHAPTER 13

It's Business, It's Always Personal

This idea that business isn't personal is total BS.
Business is personal.
—Marcus Lemonis

All of us, at some point in our careers, have probably heard management utter the mantra, "it's not personal, it's business." And if we weren't the intended recipients of this dreaded phrase, we may know someone who was, or we have seen or heard of situations where this has happened. This expression frequently appears when superiors mistreat employees and attempt to justify their actions by pretending that the dynamics of human relationships are radically different at work. They are not. Human beings work in these companies, institutions, and organizations. Employees don't abandon their humanity when they enter their workplaces.

When managers use this expression, they indirectly acknowledge that such conduct would not be acceptable in normal interactions with others. But since this is at work, they believe they'll get a pass. They feel justified treating individuals in an inconsiderate manner. In the name of business they behave unethically or indecently, then distance themselves from taking responsibility for their offensive behavior. They hide behind the organization. They pretend they don't know how this effects employees. They assume their justification that *it's not personal, it's business* somehow excuses their behavior. It doesn't. If the same phrase was directed at them, those higher-ups would take it most personally. If the shoe was on the other foot, it would suddenly become extremely personal. Why would it be any different when the person at the receiving end of the conversation is an employee?

Real Management Philosophy: "We'll Sacrifice You to Protect Ourselves"

If you work for an organization where management practices the *it's not personal, it's business* philosophy—and their words and actions support it—there's a virtual certainty that individuals already are or will be treated poorly. It's another indicator of organizational dysfunction and incompetence. Managers are signaling that they cannot be trusted to have your back when economic troubles and business or financial problems arise. You won't be able to count on them to protect you (or at least not hurt you), no matter how long you've worked there, or how experienced, loyal, and productive you are. They will easily cut your salary or destroy your career since it's only "business" after all. You're not a real person to them, you're just a number.

When exhibiting the "it's just business" mentality, executives reveal that their true loyalties lie with themselves, not anyone else inside the company. Of course, higher-ups will pretend that it's all "for the good of the organization," when they devalue and mistreat employees. That's just a smoke screen. In reality, executives are saying that they're willing to sacrifice anyone to insure they get to keep their jobs. They're focusing on their own enrichment and survival at the expense of their employees and even their customers. It's ultimately about them and their own positions and salaries. They could care less about you. They know it, and now you know it.

Every Organization is in the People Business

Every organization is in the people business, in the human relationships business. It hires, trains, and promotes people. Those employees continually interact and collaborate with more people, co-workers, to help or provide services or products to other people, the customers. And if an organization is not a for-profit business, usually its objective is to serve people who need aid, support, or assistance. Supervisors, managers, directors, executives, vice presidents, and CEOs lead, manage, mentor, and discipline people. A company's employees also partner with and depend on people from other organizations who provide services or products necessary to support the company's internal processes and operations. They are all in the people business.

This should be simple and obvious to everyone, especially to the highly educated and well compensated individuals who are in charge and have the power and ability to act accordingly. Yet even leaders of government agencies, public schools, universities, charitable foundations, and religious institutions forget or ignore that they're in the people business. The callousness and indifference with which higher-ups treat other human beings, even the most innocent and vulnerable among us, is both shocking and sickening. Human lives are being adversely affected and needless human suffering ensues due to the selfishness, greed, or apathy of management. Those who have the authority and power—and high salaries, many benefits, and guaranteed pensions—to take corrective action and do the right thing, simply don't.

It's Not Personal, It's Just Government

Every day, foster care children continue to be subjected to unacceptable emotional, physical, and sexual abuse.

—Andrew Ritholz

There are countless examples of governmental and social services agencies that are managed incompetently and recklessly, leading to the preventable pain and torment of innocent human beings. These organizations are entrusted to protect children, assist the sick, help veterans, and aid the elderly, but frequently fail to accomplish their duties. Children, the most vulnerable and defenseless members of our society, are often the victims of this management travesty.

Every year, thousands of foster children are neglected and abused while under the supervision of government-run social service agencies. According to attorney Andrew Ritholz, a comprehensive review of abuses in the foster care system from 2004 "cited findings that 28% of children in the Maryland foster care system had suffered abuse." Other states showed similar rates, "with a 21% abuse rate in foster care homes in Louisiana, and a 25% rate in Missouri." Ritholz further observes that various organizations have also studied system-wide foster care abuses and "have concluded that children in state care are *10 times* more likely to be abused than children in the care of their biological parents."

"While the limited data available about foster care abuse is shocking, inside stories suggest that the problem may be much worse than what is actually reported. Even though child welfare services has systems and requirements in place for monitoring foster care and visiting foster homes, these safeguards don't always happen or fail to detect abuse when it is occurring. Every day, foster care children continue to be subjected to unacceptable emotional, physical, and sexual abuse," concludes Ritholz. Meanwhile the "public servants" who run these agencies conduct business as usual. They display an appalling disregard for the safety and well-being of these children, since "it's just business, it's just government" after all. Those in charge—the only ones who can actually do something about it—don't even bother to try to change anything anymore. They accept that incompetence and mediocrity are permanently institutionalized. They shrug their shoulders and whine: "it's not personal, it's just government."

Many public schools are similarly mismanaged by well-paid academics and career bureaucrats. While claiming they "care about the children," they repeatedly fail to properly educate them, discipline them, and substantively teach them basic knowledge and skills. In some school districts a significant number of students are allowed to graduate functionally illiterate. Despite spending 12 years of their lives being "taught" in those schools, these teens reach adulthood without basic English reading and writing skills, and without acquiring essential math and science skills. "According to The Literacy Project, there are currently 45 million Americans who are functionally illiterate, unable to read above a 5th grade level, and half of all adults can't read a book at an

8th grade level. In California, 25 percent of the state's 6 million students are unable to perform basic reading skills," warns Larry Sand, a former classroom teacher and president of the non-profit, no-partisan, and non-political California Teachers Empowerment Network.

Public school teachers who truly care about these students and desire to effectively address this catastrophe are not given the authority or resources to do what's required. Meanwhile, mediocre and incompetent academics and educators who simply maintain the status quo are protected and tolerated. Yes, parents also share a great deal of the responsibility, but this doesn't excuse the irresponsible behavior and repeated failures of public school administrators who are entrusted to educate these children and prepare them for the real world.

When dealing with other people's children "it's just business." But if it was the public school teachers' own children, it "would be personal." Perhaps this is why so many of these teachers, officials, and administrators send their own children to private schools. Based on a study by Thomas B. Fordham Institute, public school teachers send their own children to private schools at a rate nearly twice the national average. In some cities that rate rises three to four times higher than the national average.

Everything in Business is Personal
Why do people leave teams and organizations? The number one reason people leave jobs is because they fail to connect with their bosses as leaders and as people.
—Jim Welch

Everything in business is personal. It begins with the key relationships between employees and customers. A company will be successful and profitable only if its customers are satisfied and happy with its product(s) or service(s); that's personal. Customer service is personal. How employees treat customers before and after a sale, is personal. Every single contact between a company's employees and its customers is personal. All relationships between management and employees are personal. All interactions between co-workers are personal. And it doesn't end there. This also applies to all relationships between the owners of the business and management and all employees. It finally extends to all contacts between the employees of an organization with other employees who work for external entities like manufacturers, suppliers, vendors, distributors, and retailers; it's all personal.

All organizations depend on healthy human interactions and relationships built on trust, integrity, and mutual respect to accomplish anything. It is human beings we work, communicate, and cooperate with continually in all professional settings across every single company, organization, and institution. The moment management forgets this truth, trouble will follow and problems will appear. The harder they try to pretend that "it's not personal," the worse things will become. You cannot ignore the human dimension of relationships and expect to effectively lead, motivate, help, and inspire people. It's impossible.

How to Protect Yourself

- If management in your current workplace believes in or practices the "it's not personal, it's business" your job is not safe, even if you have a long track record of excellence. You are ultimately just a number to them. Be careful and consider alternate plans for your future.

- Use the additional advice and recommendations provided in this book to determine the right strategies to follow, find a better organization to work for, or think about starting your own business.

- Also review the guidance provided in the "How to Protect Yourself" section at the end of Chapter 10, as it's relevant to this situation.

Apply and Remember

- Everything in business is always personal.

- Every organization is in the people business.

- Every organization is in the human relationships business.

- You work and interact with real people in all workplace situations, therefore act accordingly.

- Treat human beings at work with the same consideration you would treat others in your personal life.

- Create work and business relationships based on mutual trust and respect with co-workers and customers.

- Never use the cliché "it's not personal, it's business," to justify inconsiderate or inappropriate behavior in any workplace situations.

- Build rapport with the human beings you interact with on a daily basis in your organization.

- Have empathy for co-workers and employees you manage and lead.

CHAPTER 14

Employees: An Organization's Most Precious Resources

*Leadership is the stewardship of the precious lives
that come to you by people walking through your door
and agreeing to share their gifts with you.*
—Bob Chapman

In the preceding chapters we focused on how organizations often demotivate and abuse employees. We reviewed multiple examples of how management mistreats human beings. In this chapter we'll examine how people should be treated in the workplace.

Employees are a company's most important assets. Employees are an organization's most valuable and precious resources. They should be cared for like family; managed responsibly, justly, and equitably; and appreciated and respected. Employees have to know they matter. Leaders must build relationships based on integrity, trust, and mutual understanding with the individuals they lead. Leaders need to demonstrate in concrete ways that people are valued in their organizations. Management should always remember that employees—especially engaged, loyal, smart, productive, and responsible ones—make a company successful, generate superior profits, and provide the best possible competitive and sustainable advantages.

Employees who are treated well, see that they matter, know their jobs are secure, trust that management will have their backs, are paid fairly, and are respected by their leaders, will be more happy, engaged, hard-working, productive, and loyal. They will literally give it their all and strive to go above-and-beyond, safe in the knowledge that what they do counts, management appreciates what they offer, and the company genuinely cares about them—and has a vested interest in their success and well-being.

Why should business owners, managers, and executives care? Why treat employees decently and ethically? Why handle employees as their most valuable resources? Because it's the right thing to do. It boosts employee morale and productivity, creates happy customers, and increases revenues. It's also very profitable.

It's the Right Thing to Do

*The truth of the matter is that you always know
the right thing to do. The hard part is doing it.*
—Norman Schwarzkopf

Human beings work in all these companies and organizations. They are not machines or robots. These men and women have hearts, minds, and souls. They have hopes and dreams. They spend most of their waking hours at work (sometimes more time than they spend with their own families) helping a company be successful and profitable, insuring an organization runs properly and effectively. They have to be properly appreciated, respected, recognized, and compensated. They deserve to be treated fairly and kindly. It's the right thing to do, it's the most ethical and wise way to manage and lead employees. (And it's also the most efficient and profitable way to lead others!)

Behind every paycheck there's a human soul. Behind that soul there's often an entire family that depends on that individual for care, love, safety, and security. When executives do right by that employee, they do right by that entire family. When management fails to do what's right, it affects not just one person, but an entire family.

It Boosts Employee Morale and Productivity

Employees who believe that management is concerned about them as a whole person—not just an employee—are more productive, more satisfied, more fulfilled. Satisfied employees mean satisfied customers, which leads to profitability.
—Anne M. Mulcahy

Employees who are treated well and compensated equitably become and remain happy, connected, and engaged employees. They also care more about their jobs and their organizations and work harder. Connected and engaged individuals are more productive employees. According to the McKinsey Global Institute, productivity can improve by 20-25% in organizations with connected employees. Gallup research has also shown that teams with highly engaged employees are 21% more productive. Another Gallup analysis of 1.4 million employees, revealed that organizations with a high level of engagement reported 22% higher productivity.

"Engaged employees are more present and productive;

they are more attuned to the needs of customers; and they are more observant of processes, standards and systems," observe Jim Harter and Annamarie Mann when referencing numerous Gallup data analyses. Yet another poll conducted by Partners In Leadership in 2018 showed that happier employees in the workplace provide additional organizational benefits. According to their data, 85% of happy employees said "they take more initiative," 73% said "they are better collaborators," and 48% said they cared "more about their work."

Improved employee morale and increased employee productivity are important because they ultimately lead to long-term profitability and value creation. They promote sustainable growth and organizational success. "Machinery can increase productivity in measurable increments, and new processes can create significant efficiencies. However, only people can stun you with quantum leaps. Only people can do ten times what even they thought they could," asserts Bob Chapman. As multiple Gallup studies have also confirmed, "engaged employees produce better business outcomes than other employees do—across industries, company sizes and nationalities, and in good economic times and bad."

It Creates Happy Customers and Increases Revenues

If you treat your staff well, they will be happy. Happy staff are proud staff, and proud staff deliver excellent customer service, which drives business success.
—Richard Branson

Happy employees inevitably create happy customers. Happy

employees produce quality products and deliver excellent services. Happy employees care about and treat customers better; they are much more likely to consistently deliver superior customer service. Happy and engaged employees help to continually meet and exceed their customers' expectations, the most important rule in business (see Chapter 7) that helps a company be profitable and successful for the long term.

Happy customers become repeat customers. Satisfied customers become loyal, lifelong customers. This increases sales and grows revenues. Happy customers become passionate brand advocates. They freely praise—in private and in public—all great businesses and their caring employees. They tell their family and friends about the excellent customer service they receive. Happy customers write positive evaluations of quality products and services. They post glowing reviews about their great experiences. They become voluntary walking and talking marketing and advertising representatives for those companies that genuinely care about them as people, before and after a sale is completed. All of these positive consequences further boost sales, increase revenues, and strengthen the long-term competitiveness of a business.

It's Very Profitable

Management's job is to take care of employees. The employees' job is to take care of the customers. Happy customers take care of the shareholders. It's a virtuous circle.
—John Mackey

Happy employees always lead to happy customers, which inevitably create happy owners and happy shareholders. The more content and productive human beings a company employs, the more profitable it will be, the more value it will generate for the long term to reward its business owners and stockholders. This virtuous cycle benefits everyone, especially the company owners. Gallup's extensive multi-year research studies consistently show that "the behaviors of highly engaged business units result in 21% greater profitability."

During the years when Barry-Wehmiller Companies—a $3 billion global technology, engineering, and IT consulting corporation with 12,000 team members—consistently practiced its "truly human leadership," which focused on properly caring for and empowering their employees, it achieved extraordinary results. As CEO Bob Chapman indicated, Barry-Wehmiller grew "by about 20% a year since 1988 and created shareholder value in excess of 15% compound a year, when the S&P 500 in that same period of time since 1988 has only created 3% percent value."

In her book, *Make More Money by Making Your Employees Happy*, clinical psychologist and business and trial consultant Noelle C. Nelson documents how profitable and beneficial appreciated employees are to a company's bottom line. She cites a study from the Jackson Organization which shows that "companies that effectively appreciate employee value enjoy a return on equity and assets more than triple that experienced by firms that don't."

Dr. Nelson highlights the benefits that Alcoa (Aluminum Company of America), its employees, and shareholders reaped after Paul O'Neill became CEO in 1987 and announced that his sole priority was "to increase worker safety." Prior to O'Neil's hiring almost every Alcoa plant averaged at least one accident per week. The fearless CEO followed through on his promise. Many investors who immediately sold their shares later regretted their decision, when the company's value and profitability subsequently skyrocketed.

"O'Neill's intense commitment to worker safety, implemented in practical, immediate and uncompromising ways, transformed the company such that within a year, Alcoa's profits hit a record high. Employee productivity soared as accident rates decreased from one accident per week in just about every Alcoa plant, to some plants going years without losing a single workday to an accident," writes Nelson. During the next 13 years, under O'Neil's leadership, Alcoa's annual income increased by 500%. "By the time O'Neill retired in 2000, the company's annual net income was five times larger than before he arrived, and its market capitalization had risen by $27 billion," writes Charles Duhigg in his book, *The Power of Habit*. If someone had purchased a million dollars worth of Alcoa's stock on the day O'Neill was hired and held on to those shares for the next 13 years, that investor "would have earned another million dollars in dividends while he [O'Neil] headed the company, and the value of their stock would be five times bigger when he left," remarks Duhigg.

The Facts Are Irrefutable

All of these examples, substantive data, and research confirm that by "putting the employee first, the customer effectively comes first by default, and in the end, the shareholder comes first by default as well," as Richard Branson correctly states. "An appreciated employee is an engaged employee. An appreciated employee is a happy employee. And happy, engaged employees translate into making more money," Noelle Nelson concludes in her well-documented book. The facts are irrefutable and the case is clear: management has to properly appreciate and treat their employees in order for any company to be profitable, competitive, and successful for the long term.

Unfortunately, this obvious principle is frequently overlooked in too many companies and organizations. As we've seen in a previous chapter, the pervasive attitude towards employees is summarized by the phrase: "You are all disposable." While company owners, managers, and executives may pay lip service to the idea that employees are valuable and important, management's behaviors and attitudes say otherwise. Employees are often taken for granted, abused, exploited, or treated as if they don't matter. Executives mistreat and mismanage their most precious resources in the worst possible ways.

I hope you see and understand even more clearly why I wrote that a revolution is needed (see Chapter 2) to address this travesty; a revolution that frees you from these dysfunctional organizations and either compels them to change or brings about their demise. They are not worthy of your hard work, trust, and loyalty; they're not worthy of any of it. They haven't earned it. They don't appreciate it. They don't deserve it.

How This Information Helps You

The information provided in this chapter can help you in several ways. First, it lays out a solid and indisputable case for why organizations should appreciate and treat employees with great care. You can reference and cite this data to address problems and try to improve your current workplace—if management is open and willing to listen and change, and you will not be punished for speaking out.

Second, you can utilize the information provided to compare with how managers and executives in your current workplace treat employees. It will indicate whether the company leadership genuinely cares about employees or only pretends to. Use the exercise below to asses where your current organization stands.

Third, based on how you evaluate your present workplace, you can determine if there are opportunities for improvement and there's a future for you with the company. It will allow you to plan accordingly. Either stay and make things better where you work now, or plan for your departure and find a caring organization that closely practices the principles covered in this chapter.

Finally, if you already own your own business or hold an executive-level position in a company and are already doing what this chapter advises, I encourage you to stay the course. You're doing the right things. On the other hand, if you are not following or are only practicing a few of the approaches covered, start making changes. Adjust, improve, and sharpen your leadership style and strategies to insure your organization treats its employees as its most valuable resources.

EXERCISE

Determine How Your Organization Views Employees

Review the following statements and compare them with how you (and others) are treated and have been treated in your current workplace. Be as fair and objective as possible to insure an accurate evaluation. Count how many "Yes" answers you have given and compare your total to the evaluation key below.

1. My manager cares for me as a human being, and his/her actions frequently corroborate this.

2. My company cares for my well-being and work accomplishments, as well as my co-workers' well-being and work accomplishments.

3. The executives and leaders of my organization treat employees as the their most valuable resources and their behavior and attitudes consistently support this principle.

4. My manager respects me as a person and has my best interests in mind.

5. My organization has repeatedly shown me that I matter as a person.

6. The work that I do is important and appreciated by management.

7. I am allowed and encouraged to do my best work in my current position.

8. I am being paid fairly and proportionally based on the work that I do.

9. I have been properly recognized and appreciated for doing excellent work in my current position.

10. Managers and executives encourage me to offer suggestions and constructive feedback to help the organization and improve things at work.

11. I have been given the resources and tools I need to do my job properly.

12. My supervisor helps me do my job better and provides useful support when needed.

13. I feel safe and secure in my current position.

14. I trust my manager will do what's in my best interest at work.

15. I know my manager will defend me if I'm unjustly accused or attacked.

16. I trust senior executives to have my manager's back and my back if needed.

17. I know that I have a future career path with my organization if I continue to do excellent work, deliver results, and provide value.

Evaluation Key and Advice

15-17 Yes answers – You work for a **great** organization. The company treats employees as its most valuable resources. People are valued and appreciated. Employees are compensated fairly and given the resources and freedom needed to do their jobs. Management truly cares about employees and will do everything to have their backs and protect their jobs. This is an excellent organization to work for and grow with.

12-14 Yes answers – You work for a **good** organization. Employees are mostly valued and appreciated. Management is doing a decent job in protecting and helping employees. Keep an eye on how things develop. There are a few signs that management is slipping. If the environment improves and more positive changes happen you, then you'll be ok. If things get worse, then start digging your tunnel and be ready to look for another job.

7-11 Yes answers – You work for an **average** organization. There are some good and bad things happening. More signs are beginning to appear that management doesn't care about employees and jobs may not be safe. Be careful and observe where the company is headed. Start considering alternative career paths at another organization. Meanwhile, get busy digging your tunnel since there are enough troublesome signs that the organization no longer treats employees as its most valuable assets.

4-6 Yes answers – You work for a **dysfunctional** organization. Employees are not valued or appreciated. Management considers individuals as just another disposable asset to use and discard at will. There's no future for you in such an organization. Accelerate your tunnel digging. Increase your networking and job search activities. Plan to leave before the organization turns toxic.

0-3 Yes answers – You work for a **toxic** organization. The death spiral has reached its final phase. It's time to leave. It's unhealthy and harmful to work in such a terrible environment. The detrimental effects on your mental, physical, and spiritual well-being outweigh any potential benefits of staying. Quit as soon as you can.

Note: This exercise is not scientific. Each of the 17 different statements are not created equal. Some are more important than others, especially given each person's individual situation and priorities. Therefore, when counting your "Yes" answers be cognizant of that fact and take it into consideration when completing your evaluation.

CHAPTER 15

Modern Feudalism:
Fixed Salary, Unlimited Hours

A lot of us have been taught that you've made it
professionally when you get paid a salary instead of an
hourly rate. That belief is not quite a scam, but it's close!
—Liz Ryan

A critical and necessary component of ethically leading and managing employees is compensating them fairly based on the work they do and the value they bring to a company. Too often, this vital aspect of effective human leadership is missing. While executives pay lip service to properly "appreciating their employees" they don't adjust the organization's employee evaluation, reward, and compensation processes to insure individuals are paid proportionally and equitably. Instead of paying employees capitalistically, many companies compensate them feudalistically.

The proper and capitalistic way to compensate and reward employees is another topic that was never substantively addressed in my formal undergraduate and graduate education in American universities. It was also never honestly discussed or fairly practiced in any of the large corporations and universities where I've worked, taught, and consulted. I learned this lesson on my own, the hard way; after spending many years donating an excessive amount of my time, energy, and efforts with little to no corresponding benefits or rewards.

As an immigrant to the United States, I was repeatedly told that I must work as hard and as long as required to get the job done, even when I wasn't paid adequately for my extra efforts. I was instructed to sacrifice personal time and put in overtime without any additional compensation to insure that my company succeeded. "That's what it takes to have a job. That's *capitalism*," I was taught. "You must pay your dues," I was reminded. "That's how a free-market economy works," I was informed. And for several decades I believed it. I faithfully followed and accepted the "fixed salary, unlimited hours" mentality as capitalistic and normal. As it turns out, it is neither. The *fixed salary, unlimited hours* philosophy is a distortion of free-market economic principles. It's abnormal. It's not true capitalism. It's feudalism.

Employee Compensation Models

Organizations will either pay employees by the hour or pay them fixed salaries. Hourly workers are paid overtime (1.5 times the normal hourly rate) for all work done beyond the eight hours per day threshold or once they work 40 hours per week—depending on each state's overtime rules. Some states have daily overtime rules while others have weekly overtime regulations. For example, in California, Nevada, and Alaska employees are paid overtime (150% the regular hourly rate) for any time worked past eight hours in a day. California employees are paid double time (200% the regular hourly rate) after they reach 12 hours worked in a day. In Kansas, however, workers are entitled to overtime pay only after they have worked 46 hours in a week.

All other things being equal, hourly employees are generally compensated more equitably, as long as individuals with comparable experience and expertise are similarly evaluated and compensated for their productivity and the quality of work they deliver. Hourly workers get paid for every minute of work they provide an organization. They are also paid for working weekends and for being "on-call" (available to work on short notice). In a sense, hourly workers are compensated semi-capitalistically, or at least not feudalistically.

Salaried employees, on the other hand, are paid a fixed amount regardless of how many hours they work per day or per week. They are not entitled to overtime premiums. They have to work weekends or during holidays if required by their managers. They don't get paid extra if they work late nights, take work home, or deal with job-related texts, emails, or phone calls while not in the office. They also are not compensated for being on-call. Some salaried employees have to work even when they're on vacation! (I recall multiple instances in my career when I spent many unpaid hours on my phone or my computer working while on vacation.)

Thankfully, good companies with decent management generally don't abuse salaried employees. Individuals are given sufficient flexibility to complete their daily tasks and projects without working overtime. Employees can typically start and leave the office at reasonable times. Employees occasionally have to put in extra hours to finish their work; but when they do, ethical managers give them time off (or other benefits) as compensation for the additional time worked.

Modern Feudalism, Neo-Feudalism

Not to put too fine a point on it, if you're working 100 hours a week while being paid for 40 hours, you should listen carefully for the sound of a power tool and trumpet fanfare, because you're being royally screwed.

—Geoffrey James

Unfortunately, dysfunctional and toxic organizations frequently set unreasonable deadlines and give salaried employees more work than they could possibly finish in 40 hours per week, forcing individuals to work overtime. Employees are pressured to "get it done" regardless of how much personal or family time is sacrificed in the process. Individuals are not rewarded in any reasonable manner for the extra hours they put in. Management never reciprocates by giving employees any time off to recompense them for the overtime worked. The only additional "benefit" employees receive is "keeping their jobs."

Unless organizations provide salaried employees performance-based bonuses, comparable time off, or other benefits that proportionally pay them for the overtime hours worked, the *fixed salary, unlimited hours* scheme is akin to *modern feudalism* or *neo-feudalism*. The employees' time and an unreasonable portion of their private lives are controlled by the organization. Individuals don't own their personal time outside the 40 hours per week, the company does; just like serfs in the middle ages didn't own the land they were working on, the feudal lords did.

Rather than treat employees as free and autonomous human beings, executives treat them like serfs. The *fixed salary, unlimited hours* philosophy signals to employees that the company in a sense "owns them," hence my decision to characterize it as *feudalism*. This abusive approach has little to do with capitalism, free-enterprise, or free-market economic principles. As a matter of fact, it's the opposite of how ethical capitalism requires companies to treat employees as their most precious and valuable resources (see Chapter 14). It's also fundamentally different from the capitalistic manner in which the executives themselves are compensated.

Capitalism for Thee, But Not for Me

Executives are usually the only people in a company who are paid capitalistically. They enjoy not only generous fixed salaries and multi-year employment contracts that protect their jobs, but also receive annual cash bonuses, profit-sharing, stock options, stock grants, performance shares, restricted stock, enhanced benefits packages, and other unique perks reserved solely for them.

Executives also have the special privilege of Golden Parachutes, they're rewarded when they are let go. Some still get paid handsomely despite causing massive financial losses or running the company into the ground. Interestingly enough, being rewarded for incompetence, recklessness, or failure is not capitalistic in any way, shape, or form. As a matter of fact, it's anti-capitalistic. It's wrong. It's misguided, unethical, and destructive.

There is nothing wrong with executives being rewarded for excellence and sharing in the success they bring to a corporation. Superior knowledge, wisdom, and expertise has to be fairly compensated. Great leadership requires unique sets of skills and abilities. It requires consistent effort and focus. It demands continued vigilance and discipline. That's why only highly qualified, wise, and experienced men and women of character and integrity can lead employees effectively, deliver consistent profitability, and insure the long-term competitiveness and growth of an organization. The deserve to be paid generously for their hard work. These executives should share in the prosperity of the company, but so should all those employees who also contribute to that process and help the company achieve that success.

In the next chapter I will describe how organizations use your ethics against you to avoid paying you proportionally and fairly. Then in Chapter 17 I will explain how employees should be compensated so they also benefit from genuine capitalistic and free-market principles.

Apply and Remember

- Companies need to fairly evaluate and adequately pay employees for the work they do and the hours they spend in the workplace.

- Organizations have to compensate employees proportionally for their productivity, the value they create, and their unique contributions toward the organization's long-term success.

- Paying employees a fixed salary and making them work unlimited hours is modern feudalism, not capitalism.

- Companies should avoid two-tiered compensation schemes where only the upper-tier executives and senior managers benefit capitalistically from the company's success, while all other lower-tier employees are paid fixed salaries.

- Organizations cannot reward anyone for incompetence, recklessness, or failure.

- There is nothing wrong with amply rewarding executives and employees for their expertise, hard work, productivity, and excellence.

CHAPTER 16

Using Your Ethics Against You

If the company can make us feel like they care for us,
then we must reciprocate to rebalance the account.
—Lucio Buffalmano

Another way organizations take advantage of you is by using your ethics against you. Management appeals to your decent nature, willingness to be a team player, and desire to be appreciated for your efforts, to persuade you to work for less money than you merit based on your actual expertise and performance. Executives use emotional appeals to manipulate and silence you when you bring up concerns about unfair workloads or inequitable pay situations you discover inside the organization.

To illustrate how inequity can happen I have crafted two different scenarios you may encounter. In both instances your assessments need to be grounded in reality and supported by the facts. Your evaluations of your own and your co-workers' productivity and work quality should be objective and unbiased.

Scenario 1 – You Are 25% More Productive
Than Co-Workers

You've worked in a company for a couple of years and you're doing a great job. You're happy with your position and pay. Then, you begin to notice that compared with other co-workers (with comparable job functions) you get about 25% more done each week, while delivering similar and even better results. You realize that you're 25% more productive than everyone else in your department. You also consistently deliver higher quality work.

Scenario 2 – New Employee Gets Hired and
Makes 25% More Than You

You've been employed by your organization for a few years and you're doing a wonderful job. Your functional role requires intense work and knowledge of multiple operational areas and processes. Over the last few years you have received, on average, a three percent annual salary increase. You're satisfied with your position. Then, a new employee gets hired to do similar work. Given the complex nature and technical requirements of the job, your organization has to offer a much higher salary to find qualified candidates for this position. After a few weeks, by a stroke of luck, you discover that the newly-hired employee is making 25% more than you for doing exactly the same kind of work you do. The new employee also has similar education, experience, and knowledge as you.

Faced with either of the two scenarios presented above, you would rightly be puzzled and concerned. If you're like me, you would approach your manager and present your case with support from evidence that you've gathered. You would sensibly outline the reasons for bringing this up and back them up with facts. You would then ask your boss to address this unfair situation and find a reasonable way to correct the noticeable inequity.

Healthy Organizations and
Fair Management Response

Fairness in the office simply means applying the rules fairly, equally, and without regards for workplace political alliances.
—John Hoover

In healthy organizations a fair manager would take you seriously. He or she would listen to you, review your documentation, and verify your conclusions. Then, your boss would act to correct the inequity and make sure your workload and compensation are properly aligned with the workloads and salaries of other co-workers doing similar jobs. You would probably get a solid raise to account for your higher productivity and quality of work. The matter would be settled fairly quickly. You would receive confirmation that your manager and company truly cared about you. You would see that ethical treatment of employees and fair practices are the norm across the organization.

Actually, in truly healthy companies neither of the two highlighted scenarios will happen. Managers and executives in great organizations regularly scrutinize their compensation models, in addition to the productivity and quality of work of their employees. They proactively monitor internal equity to ensure everyone is fairly evaluated and paid. If unreasonable workloads or inequitable pay situations do occur, bosses act swiftly to rectify the unfairness and restore equity.

Dysfunctional Organizations and Unfair Management Response

Corporations lie and manipulate. HR lies and manipulates. And your boss lies and manipulates.

—Lucio Buffalmano

Managers and executives in dysfunctional and toxic organizations have a much different reaction. When you approach them with your concerns and provide evidence of the inequity you uncovered, they typically respond in any one of a number of ways. They:

1. **Tell you that it's none of your business.** They admonish you for being nosy. They lecture you on not comparing yourself with others. They accuse you of stirring up trouble. They insist that only management is qualified to handle these matters. They tell you to mind your own business and ignore what's going on.

2. **Lie to you and tell you it's not true.** They deny the truth of what's happening. They dismiss the information you provide as unreliable or false. They lie to your face and expect you to accept their lies as truth.

3. **Make excuses or rationalize away the unfairness.** If the previous two tactics don't persuade you to give up, managers come up with all sorts of phony reasons why the inequity exists or why it can't be corrected. This is an indirect admission that you're right, but managers never acknowledge that. Instead, they either challenge your own performance and quality of work, or artificially enhance the accomplishments and productivity of the co-workers you referenced, or concoct some other explana-

tion to shut you up. They also claim that their hands are tied and there's nothing they can do about it. They pretend that redressing the inequity is not up to them, that it's someone else's decision to make. They continually come up with bogus excuses to explain or rationalize away the unfair treatment.

4. **Attempt to shame you into silence.** If you stubbornly continue to ask for a reasonable solution, bosses deploy the shaming routine. They lament how disappointed they are in you. They scold you for being selfish. They rebuke you for only caring about money. They say that you are not a team player or don't appreciate your job. They accuse you of being ungrateful for the opportunity they've given you. They remind you of how lucky you are to work for the organization.

Managers Use Your Ethics Against You

It's not employees who matter,
it's the output of the employees that matters.
—Dan Rust

When you attempt to correct an unfair work situation and management responds with the absurd accusations, lies, and excuses mentioned above, know that you're being played for a fool. Managers emotionally manipulate you to make you acquiesce to their demands and give up the quest for a just and equitable resolution. They appeal to your decency and good nature to make you accept unfairness as normal. Bosses use your ethics against you. They hoodwink you into donating 25% of your hard work to the organization.

Managers expect you to sacrifice, while they don't lift a

finger to help. After all, management will continue to benefit from the additional 25% productivity you deliver while the company underpays you. Executives keep costs down, boost profits, and get better bonuses and raises for themselves; while you donate a quarter of your efforts. It's a win-win for management and the organization. It's a lose-lose for you. It's unethical and wrong on every level.

Don't Let Them Use Your Ethics Against You
People who truly understand what is meant by self-reliance know they must live their lives by ethics rather than rules.
—Wayne Dyer

Faced with dysfunctional managers who refuse to help and do what's right, you will have to restore equity on your own. If your boss is not going to look out for you, you must fend for yourself. This is ethical and right. Since you deliver 25% more value to your company than other co-workers while getting paid the same, it's unfair to continue in this manner.

Assuming you like your job and don't want to leave, or cannot presently quit your job, here's what you should do. Gradually reduce the pace and intensity of your work until it roughly matches the workload and productivity of your co-workers. Do it stealthily and quietly. Don't tell anyone in the company what you're doing. Make sure it's slow enough that your boss and co-workers do not notice. You don't want to attract their attention, especially if you've already spoken with your boss or co-workers about the unfair treatment.

Maintain the same quality of your work as before. It's the ethical way to go. You cannot adversely impact the quality of the product(s) or service(s) you're responsible for and the company provides to others. It will reflect badly on you and negatively affect innocent people. Additionally, you don't want to give your boss a reason to reprimand or fire you.

If you have more freedom to work independently or there's less scrutiny of your daily schedule and work area, then you can maintain the same pace and intensity. However, you owe the company only six hours of work each day. The remaining two hours (25% of the workday) belong to you. Ethically the company is not entitled to them. You deliver the same quality results in six hours that other employees complete in eight hours. Why should you donate two more hours of your life when the organization refuses to pay for your greater productivity? It's inequitable. It's unjust. It's feudalistic, it's not capitalistic.

The additional energy and time you have ethically rescued from a dysfunctional workplace are yours. Never be ashamed to save them for yourself. Use them as you see fit to help you and your future. Invest them to improve your skills, enhance your knowledge, boost your health, reduce your stress, recharge, start a side business, launch a new business, or dig your tunnel to escape; then seek better opportunities with another company that will pay you fairly for the higher productivity you bring. This is ethical. This is just. This is free-market capitalism.

Apply and Remember

- Dysfunctional organizations use your ethics against you. They don't compensate you fairly for your higher productivity or greater responsibilities.

- Managers and executives in healthy organizations regularly scrutinize their compensation models, and their employees' productivity and quality of work to insure everyone is fairly evaluated and paid.

- Abusive bosses refuse to correct unfair work situations and respond with absurd accusations, lies, and excuses. They emotionally manipulate you to give up the quest for a just and equitable resolution and acquiesce to their demands.

- Never let bosses use your ethics against you.

- When faced with dysfunctional managers who refuse to help and do what's right, you will have to restore equity on your own.

- Reduce your pace and intensity at work to approximately match the workload and productivity of your co-workers who do similar work.

- The additional energy and time you have ethically rescued from a dysfunctional workplace are yours. Never be ashamed to save them for yourself. This is free-market capitalism.

CHAPTER 17

Microcapitalism:
Reward Employees Capitalistically

Just as important, we need a new dedication to opening avenues for employee participation and motivation through profit-sharing and innovative programs of job enrichment.
—Charles H. Percy

I use the term "microcapitalism" to identify the fair and ethical way to compensate employees capitalistically and differentiate it from the feudalistic manner in which many individuals are actually paid. Profit-sharing and stock grants are essential components of *microcapitalism*. I think it's an accurate way to describe how companies should reward individuals based on true free-market principles and give them a real stake in the business.

At a minimum, microcapitalism requires that companies allocate and distribute a portion of their profits to employees as bonuses, based on merit. This is known as profit-sharing. It's a supplementary financial incentive that individuals receive in addition to their salaries. Healthy and smart businesses typically do this already; they offer profit-sharing not only to executives, but also to managers and employees.

Furthermore, corporations should offer high-performing

employees stock grants or give them the opportunity to buy shares at a significantly discounted rate as part of their compensation. These shares would be distributed (and vested over time) to deserving employees, based on their performance and the value they bring to the company. Most corporations currently offer stock grants only to high-level executives, never to managers or other employees. Microcapitalism, however, gives all employees the opportunity to earn and receive company shares as reward for excellent work and loyal service.

Capitalism for Thee and Me:
Turn Employees Into Owners

Turn the management and as many employees as possible
into stockholders—and with enough stock
so they think of themselves as owners.
—Robert Townsend

Microcapitalism is the best way to transform great employees into part-owners of the business. It gives them a stake in the organization and incentivizes them to work harder and smarter, since their fortunes are now tied to the company's fortune. It lets them have skin in the game. It's an effective way to motivate employees to take greater ownership of their functional roles and care more about the company and its customers; since happy customers increase revenues and boost profits.

Microcapitalism leads to increased productivity and greater innovation throughout the organization. It harnesses and redirects the employees' self-interest into positive and constructive energy that's dedicated into making the organization better and more profitable. It helps employees be fully engaged which greatly benefits the company. "Their level of commitment would be different. Your business will do better if you let them participate," advises Marcus Lemonis, successful serial entrepreneur, great leader, and star of the show "The Profit." Employees will become more accountable since their pay will be directly affected by their behavior at work. They will look for ways to grow the business, intelligently reduce costs, and increase profitability, since they also proportionally benefit when the company does well and are negatively impacted when the business suffers. It's no longer someone else's company, it's now truly *their* company. And that makes all the difference in the world.

Microcapitalism also helps improve company stability and workplace continuity. It minimizes human resources disruptions. It's an ethical way to retain an organization's best employees, which should ultimately be all employees (see Chapter 7). It reduces employee turnover and makes it difficult for them to quit or leave, as they now have a vested interest in the organization and its long-term success. It also makes it more challenging for competitors to poach key employees. Why would individuals leave a prosperous business that appreciates them, treats them decently, rewards them for excellence, allows them to share in the profits, makes them part-owners, and gives them opportunities for growth? They would be crazy to quit, especially since there are too many dysfunctional organizations and poorly run companies out there.

Key Characteristics of Effective Microcapitalism

Recognize that to have maximum effectiveness, profit-center-related bonuses must be computed in accordance with an accounting system which everyone understands and recognizes as fair.

—Robert Townsend

As mentioned above, microcapitalism requires profit-sharing and some form of stock grants for employees. Furthermore, a company's microcapitalistic reward and compensation plan, in order to be successful and provide maximum beneficial effects, should have the following specific characteristics:

1. **Universally applied, from the janitor to the CEO** – It should be available to everyone in the company, from entry-level employees to the highest level executives, from the janitor all the way to the CEO. It cannot be reserved exclusively for executives and senior managers; that's feudalism (see Chapter 15).

2. **Clear and easily understood** – The methods for measuring and assessing employee performance and productivity need to be clear and comprehensive— guided by objective criteria and processes. The rules for allocating profits and determining stock grants based on employee merit have to be straightforward and easily understood by everyone. There should not be any confusion regarding how or why any employee is microcapitalistically compensated.

3. **Fair and transparent** – Employee evaluation processes and profit allocation methods need to be fair and trans-

parent, and fully disclosed. Everyone has to play by the same rules. There cannot be any "special rules for special people." Employees need to trust the process and know they are all assessed objectively and rewarded fairly.

4. **No ceiling, no maximum limits** – To amplify the beneficial results of microcapitalism, the compensation of each employee cannot be limited because it has become too large. "For maximum effectiveness, no ceiling should be put on a profit-measured bonus merely because it has become substantial," writes Robert Townsend. Therefore companies cannot place maximum limits on the financial rewards employees receive based on their hard work and performance; after all, their efforts significantly contributed to the growth and prosperity of the business. Under microcapitalism, they've earned the right to share in the success of the organization, just like other stockholders.

By turning employees into engaged and accountable owners, microcapitalism ultimately transforms people into walking and talking profit and performance hawks, who continually look out for the best interests of the company (and its customers) and work toward its long-term profitability and success. Microcapitalism provides the ethical, fair, and self-correcting mechanism required to maximize employee engagement and optimize their effectiveness. It is the best way to facilitate and maintain a healthy organizational atmosphere, sustainable growth, and constant innovation. It is the wisest way to build enduring value and deliver prosperity to all those who helped create it.

Apply and Remember

- Microcapitalism requires that companies offer profit-sharing and stock grants to employees based on merit as part of their compensation.

- Giving employees a stake in the business is an effective and ethical way to motivate them to work harder and support the long-term profitability and success of a company.

- Microcapitalism should be universally and fairly applied, from entry-level employees to the highest level executives, from the janitor all the way to the CEO.

- People don't leave prosperous organizations that appreciate them, treat them decently, reward them for excellence, allow them to share in the profits, make them part-owners, and give them opportunities for growth.

- Microcapitalism is the wisest way to build enduring value and deliver prosperity to all those employees who helped create it.

CHAPTER 18

Your Boss Might Be a Sociopath

About one in twenty-five individuals are sociopathic, mean-ing, essentially, that they do not have a conscience. It is not that this group fails to grasp the difference between good and bad; it is that the distinction fails to limit their behavior.
—Martha Stout, PhD

As far-fetched as it may seem, you may work alongside a sociopath, or worse, your boss could be a psychopath. This perhaps explains the source of your dysfunctional or toxic workplace, department, or team. It may explain why you're constantly stressed, demoralized, and miserable; why you feel trapped and hopeless. As a matter of fact, it could be the reason why everything you've done to succeed in your job, be appreciated by your co-workers or superiors, and get ahead in your career has not worked.

If things keep getting worse for you the more you try to help the organization and do excellent work, there's a high likelihood that your boss exhibits sociopathic traits. If you keep getting in trouble for speaking the truth, acting ethically, and doing the right things, your manager most likely has psychopathic tendencies.

The concept that sociopaths and psychopaths lurk inside

companies, organizations, and institutions, was never taught or covered in my formal university education, at the undergraduate or graduate level. The danger these individuals pose to others, the dysfunction they spread, and the damage they do inside organizations were never addressed in any courses on management, leadership, or organizational behavior. I discovered this truth on my own after enduring many abuses and suffering repeated professional setbacks. I have paid a heavy price to learn this important lesson. Yet, this critical bit of knowledge turns out to be key in understanding the complex human dynamics of the workplace. Without it, we are unable to accurately discern what's actually going on, determine how to properly respond, and effectively protect ourselves and our livelihoods.

Something Was *Off* with People at Work

Early on in my professional career I began noticing that something was *off* with some of the people I worked with, especially managers, executives, and company owners. It didn't matter if the organization was a small business or a multi-billion dollar corporation. While many individuals seemed normal, their behavior was frequently abnormal. Many were charming and friendly at first glance. They dressed professionally and spoke intelligently (most of the time). They smiled and seemed amicable.

However, repeated interactions with these individuals revealed clues that something was not right. They were not who they professed to be. Their explanations often didn't make sense. They behaved unethically and habitually lied, but claimed they didn't. They repeatedly mistreated others, but cast themselves as victims. They emotionally manipulated and intimidated co-workers to benefit themselves, but labeled themselves as "caring." They professed to be "selfless," but careful observation of their actions showed they were selfish and self-centered.

Oftentimes the manipulations were subtle. Outward demeanors did not change. The individuals maintained a professional facade. They talked calmly and chose their words carefully. They were polite and smiled. They even cracked jokes. They didn't get angry or raise their voices. Some even cried on cue, when needed. Their actions, however, didn't match their words. Their smiles felt like forced grins. Their talk didn't match their walk. Their reactions to certain situations were out of synch with what was happening. Emotions displayed felt artificial, almost as if they were acting them out, but not really experiencing them. Even though they mouthed the right words, their body language and facial expressions seemed to be saying something else. To use a Star Wars analogy, I felt a "disturbance in the Force." I sensed there was something else always lurking just below the surface personality presented to the world.

As I changed jobs and worked and consulted for different companies, I kept encountering the same perplexing patterns of behavior from people in other institutions. The higher up the organizational structure I worked, the worse it became. Then I began teaching in universities and realized, to my amazement and disappointment, that academia was no different. The treacherous waters of academia were just as bad as the perilous waters of corporate America. I should not have been surprised. Human nature is the same regardless of environment.

Across three decades of working, consulting, and teaching, I observed that the management ranks of companies and institutions of all sizes harbored inveterate pretenders. They were masters of fake smiles and insincere declarations. They excelled in playing the "nice" game. They were epic BS artists. They could spin a story better than anyone. Their tales, however, clashed with reality, even though morsels of truth were strategically sprinkled in to lend credibility to their stories, disorient their victims, and provide cover if anyone challenged them. They re-wrote history and twisted facts with such ease and conviction that their intended targets would begin to question their own sanity.

These were not just generally unethical, egotistical, hypocritical, or arrogant individuals we typically come across. These folks specialized in duplicitous and devious conduct. They were good at hiding and disguising their real intentions. They lacked genuine compassion for others. Whatever concern they displayed didn't appear authentic. They used it to control people. They constantly manipulated, undermined, fooled, and betrayed co-workers to advance their own agendas, silence criticism, and consolidate their power. They behaved unconscionably as they played games with other people's careers and lives.

Corporate Scandals and Institutional Abuses

We've seen the hubris. And now we're seeing the scandals.
—David Gergen

There was evidence that my experiences were not unique. Something was definitely wrong with those heading other corporations and organizations in America and around the world. Since the 1990s an endless stream of corporate and institutional scandals continually filled the headlines, all caused by dysfunctional, unethical, or criminal conduct of top management. It culminated with the 2008 economic crisis that destroyed trillions of dollars in wealth and impoverished millions. That disaster was precipitated by the reckless misdeeds and wrongdoing of elites at multiple financial institutions; who were enabled by corrupt politicians in Washington, DC. (Oh yes, forgot to mention, the political class is full of these sociopaths, as I came to understand.) How was it possible that such flawed executives survived, advanced, and prospered in these corporations?

Even religious institutions were not immune. As a matter of fact, the leadership of the Catholic Church was responsible for some of the most heinous and reprehensible conduct imaginable. For decades, Catholic bishops coddled corrupt men—child rapists and molesters of boys—and allowed them to operate unhindered inside the church. These depraved priests destroyed the innocence and shattered the lives of thousands of children. Meanwhile the church hierarchy covered up the terrible sexual abuses, silenced victims, and protected the predatory priests. Shockingly, cardinals and bishops deliberately transferred pedophile priests to different parishes without warning the new congregations. Wicked human beings prowled and thrived inside these organizations. How? Why? I eventually found the answer.

Workplace Sociopaths, Hiding in Plain Sight

Many mental health professionals refer to the condition of little or no conscience as "antisocial personality disorder," a noncorrectable disfigurement of character that is now thought to be present in about 4 percent of the

population—that is to say, one in twenty-five people.
This condition of missing conscience is called by other
names, too, most often "sociopathy," or
the somewhat more familiar term, "psychopathy."
—Martha Stout, PhD

One day, I started reading *The Sociopath Next Door* book written by Martha Stout, PhD, an experienced psychologist and clinical instructor who worked in the Department of Psychiatry at Harvard Medical School for over 25 years. Dr. Stout reveals that four percent of individuals in society—one in 25 people—lack a conscience; they are sociopaths and psychopaths. They don't feel guilt, shame, or remorse. They have no empathy towards other human beings. Sociopaths will do and say anything to manipulate and control others, even if it means psychologically traumatizing or destroying the careers or lives of their victims. While sociopaths are often difficult to identify, the trails of chaos, destruction, and human suffering they generate and leave behind are unmistakable and damning.

A light bulb went on! My eyes were opened. Suddenly it all made sense. Those disturbing individuals I had met, worked with, and read about were sociopaths and psychopaths. Reflecting back at the strange and abnormal behavior I had experienced and witnessed, *sociopathy* was the best and most accurate explanation. I found the missing piece to the puzzle I had been trying to solve for years. I finally understood why sociopaths always seemed *off* and why I frequently felt "a disturbance in the Force" when dealing with them. These were spiritually dark individuals. I was sensing real evil.

Sociopaths are Hard to Identify

Very few people, no matter how educated they are in other ways, know the meaning of the word sociopathic. Far less do they understand that, in all probability, the word could be properly applied to a handful of people they actually know.

—Martha Stout, PhD

Now, why did it take me so long to figure this out? Why was it so hard to identify sociopaths and admit that they worked and lived right next to me? One reason I already mentioned. My undergraduate and graduate formal education did not cover this topic. I was wholly unaware and unprepared to deal with it. Dr. Stout provides more explanations why many of us find it difficult to spot sociopaths and acknowledge their presence in our lives, even when we're confronted with undeniable evidence of their existence.

First, we don't have a comprehensive understanding of the terminology. Clinical terms like *sociopathy* and *psychopathy* conjure up images of mentally unstable, deranged, or menacing-looking creeps who reside in mental institutions. We don't expect to find sociopaths and psychopaths sitting or living right next to us. We can't conceive that they work, attend school, socialize, spend leisure time, play sports, or live with us. We think these monsters have no place in civil society, polite company, or in professional settings, let alone in our living rooms. Yet that is precisely where we encounter most of them.

Second, we believe the stereotype that sociopaths and psychopaths are violent criminals, cold-blooded murderers, or serial killers, usually locked up in prison or sitting on death row. Or, we picture genocidal dictators like Stalin, Hitler, or Mao Zedong who mercilessly starved, tortured, and murdered tens of millions of innocent people, including many in their own inner circles. We could never imagine that average, normal-looking, and friendly—even charming—co-workers, managers, bosses, friends, or family members could be sociopathic. "But most sociopaths are not mass murderers or serial killers. They are not Pol Pot or Ted Bundy. Instead, most are only life-size, like the rest of us, and can remain unidentified for long periods of time," explains Dr. Stout.

Finally, even when we have clear evidence and suspect someone is a sociopath, we find it difficult to accept it. "Absolute guiltlessness defies the imagination," indicates Dr. Stout. For normal and decent human beings, the 96 percent of us with a conscience, it's hard to understand how a person lacks a conscience. We have no frame of reference for such evil. Our human experiences prepare us to sympathize and relate to all sorts of normal human conditions like exuberance, physical pain, or depression. We have all felt excited, dealt with bodily aches and pains, or felt despondent at times. However, not caring at all about how our actions hurt other human beings is completely alien to us. We are unable to grasp such a diabolical manner of existing.

Sociopath or Psychopath?

In my work, I use the term sociopathy, but there is no universally agreed-upon distinction between that designation and any of the others, including psychopathy.
—Martha Stout, PhD

According to the Mayo Clinic: "Antisocial personality disorder, sometimes called sociopathy, is a mental disorder in which a person consistently shows no regard for right and wrong and ignores the rights and feelings of others. People with antisocial personality disorder tend to antagonize, manipulate or treat others harshly or with callous indifference. They show no guilt or remorse for their behavior."

Dr. Stout, like other psychologists, psychiatrists, and clinicians, uses the terms "sociopath" and "psychopath" interchangeably when referring to people with "antisocial personality disorder." Since these individuals share many similar traits, it's difficult to differentiate between the two classifications. "A popular idea is that a 'psychopath' is violent and a 'sociopath' is not, but this condition is inaccurate," she observes. Both terms are used to "refer to a person who is devoid of conscience but who may or many not be prone to violence," writes Dr. Stout in her latest book, *Outsmarting the Sociopath Next Door.*

Criminologist Scott Bonn, PhD on the other hand, believes that sociopaths are more "volatile and prone to emotional outbursts, including fits of rage." He claims psychopaths tend to be "cool, calm, and meticulous," and are typically more "aggressive and predatory in nature." Dr. Bonn also asserts that psychopaths are better able to mimic emotions, which helps them more easily manipulate and control their victims. They "will appear normal to unsuspecting people," cautions Dr. Bonn.

I also think of psychopaths as more aggressive, ruthless, and dangerous sociopaths, who effortlessly control their victims with a calm demeanor and amiable facade. This is just a matter of writing style and personal preference. Since not all sociopaths are the same, I would use the psychopath label for the worst sociopaths. If it helps, you use it; if it doesn't, don't. For purposes of this book I have followed Dr. Stout's expert advice and used the terms interchangeably, to be consistent and pay deference to her professional opinion.

Top-Level Sociopaths and Psychopaths
It is not the image we like to have when we think of business leaders. But troubling research indicates that in the ranks of senior management, psychopathic behavior may be more common than we think.
—Victor Lipman

Additional research helped me understand why I kept noticing a greater concentration of sociopaths at the highest levels of organizational management. "In their professional careers, higher-functioning sociopaths and psychopaths are nakedly ambitious, shrewdly exploitative, and ruthlessly aggressive. They often maneuver their way to positions of power and status in business, finance, politics, media, and other prominent fields. They attain success at the unethical expense of using and abusing others," cautions Professor Preston Ni.

"Many of psychopaths' defining characteristics—their polish, charm, cool decisiveness, and fondness for the fast lane—are easily, and often, mistaken for leadership qualities," observes Gardiner Morse. But their charisma is frequently accompanied by other much more disturbing traits that make psychopaths more menacing and dangerous. "They're cunning, manipulative, untrustworthy, unethical, parasitic, and utterly remorseless. There's nothing they won't do, and no one they won't exploit, to get what they want," warns Morsen, based on the research of renowned criminal psychologist Robert D. Hare, PhD. In his book, *Snakes in Suits*, co-authored with Paul Babiak, PhD, Dr. Hare explains that psychopaths can easily climb the corporate ladder and be successful in business settings more often than we realize. The psychopaths' charm, highly developed social skills, and lack of conscience, allow them to ruthlessly manipulate and maneuver their way to the top, and effortlessly undermine and destroy anyone who gets in their way. When you don't have a conscience, anything goes.

Another light bulb went on! Those diabolical, yet outwardly charismatic, senior managers, executives, deans, and presidents were in all likelihood psychopaths. Once again, all the unsettling and unconscionable behavior I had seen and experienced in various companies and universities finally made sense. This was the best explanation for the real cause of many corporate and institutional scandals. I suspect that if we looked carefully for the source of most organizational dysfunction, a top-level psychopath is to blame or several high-level sociopaths are responsible.

Has Your Light Bulb Gone On?

Does any of this ring true with regards to your organization? Do you recognize some of these traits in your boss or co-workers? Are you beginning to understand what's actually happening? Do you see why you've suffered despite all your attempts to deliver good work and do the right things in your job? If yes, then you're reading the right book at the right time. It's time to defend yourself from these wicked individuals. It's time to fight back and regain your freedom.

Battle Between Good and Evil

Sociopaths are almost invariably seen as bad or diabolical, even by (or perhaps especially by) mental health

professionals, and the sentiment that these patients
are somehow morally offensive and scary
comes across vividly in the literature.
—Martha Stout, PhD

Experts maintain that sociopaths prefer to target honest, kind, loving, and generous individuals. They do this because innocent and trusting individuals can be more easily duped and manipulated; and once snared take longer to spot the evil and cruelty of their tormentors. Gentle and decent individuals also tolerate more abuse and don't fight back as fiercely as ordinary folks, giving the psychopaths more latitude to control their innocent targets.

As a matter of fact, sociopaths seem especially attracted to honorable individuals, people of strong character. Dr. Stout observes that "strong characters are often specially targeted by sociopaths." Based on her professional experience she thinks that sociopaths—despite their lack of conscience—still feel an internal void and realize they lack "something that other people have." What sociopaths actually envy, "and may seek to destroy as a part of the game, is usually something in the character structure of a person with conscience," explains Dr. Stout.

So, if you discover that you've been the target of multiple sociopaths, either at work or in your personal life, it's not necessarily your fault. Well, actually it is your fault. But the "fault" is probably a virtue, not a character flaw. Most likely your strong character, decency, trusting nature, and loving disposition attracted those sociopaths and made you more susceptible to their devious manipulations. Believe me, I speak from experience. I am one of those trusting and decent idiots who was repeatedly taken advantage of by various sociopaths. I've had more than my fair share of dealing with them. Thankfully, I have finally learned my lesson. Hopefully, after reading this book, you will too.

Never forget this is a battle between good and evil. When you defend yourself from sociopaths and fight back (wisely and strategically) against psychopaths you wage a battle against evildoers. This is a worthy endeavor. You're doing something good and honorable. In the next chapter I will cover practical advice on how to spot sociopaths and effectively protect yourself.

Apply and Remember

- Sociopaths could be the reason for your dysfunctional or toxic workplace, department, or team.

- Sociopaths look normal, even charming, from the outside and can remain hidden for long periods of time.

- Sociopaths are experts in disguising their true emotions and intentions.

- Sociopaths specialize in duplicitous and devious conduct.

- Sociopaths lack empathy for others. They see people as objects to manipulate and control as they see fit. They play games with people's careers and lives.

- Sociopathic conduct is unconscionable, it's evil.

- The psychopaths' charm, highly developed social skills, and lack of conscience, allow them to ruthlessly manipulate and maneuver their way to the top levels of organizations.

- Sociopaths are especially attracted to honorable, kind, and decent individuals, people of strong character.

- Defending yourself from sociopaths is ultimately a battle between good and evil.

- The bad news is that 4% of individuals in society are sociopaths.

- The good news is that 96% of people in society have a conscience.

CHAPTER 19

How to Spot Sociopaths
and Protect Yourself

*As a psychologist and as a person, I have seen far too many
lives nearly obliterated by the choices and acts of a
conscienceless few. These few are both dangerous and
remarkably difficult to identify.*
—Martha Stout, PhD

Detecting sociopaths is critical to your physical, mental, and
spiritual health. It's difficult, often impossible, to achieve
financial and mental freedom if you work for a sociopath and
either don't realize it or don't effectively deal with it. I included this additional chapter in the book to help you spot
sociopaths and protect yourself from their devious schemes.

Despite their normal outward appearance, sociopaths pose
a serious threat to your well-being. While most of them will
not resort to physical violence, they specialize in mental and
spiritual violence. Dr. Martha Stout warns that sociopaths
"are all too capable of mangling individual lives, and of making human society as a whole an unsafe place to be."
Remember, sociopaths don't really have a conscience. They
do not feel empathy toward others. They feel no shame and
no guilt. There's nothing to hold them in check as they play
with your life and destroy your future.

Experienced psychologists are well-acquainted with the harm done by sociopaths to other human beings. "In helping my patients and their families cope with the harm done to their lives, and in studying their case histories, I have learned that the damage caused by the sociopaths among us is deep and lasting, often tragically lethal, and startlingly common," explains Dr. Stout. She should know. Dr. Stout has spent twenty-five years working with hundreds of individuals who have suffered because of sociopaths. My own terrible encounters with sociopaths mirror Dr. Stout's experiences and confirm how dangerous sociopaths are and the havoc they wreak on the lives of innocent people.

How to Spot Sociopaths

To do something about shameless people, we must first identify them. So, in our individual lives, how do we recognize the one person out of (more or less) twenty-five who has no conscience and who is potentially dangerous to our resources and our well-being?
—Martha Stout, PhD

Sociopaths are difficult to spot. For many conscience-bound individuals most sociopaths are invisible, according to Dr. Stout. Their lack of conscience and superior ability to mimic emotions make them especially adept at hiding in plain sight and pretending to be normal. They easily blend in. They are masters of deception. This allows them to work and live in close proximity to decent individuals and remain undetected.

Sociopaths are also accomplished actors. They take on whatever roles they need to optimally manipulate and con their victims. They are so effective that even experienced psychologists can be fooled. "Everyone, including the experts, can be taken in, manipulated, conned, and left bewildered by them. A good psychopath can play a concerto on anyone's heartstrings," warns Robert D. Hare, PhD.

Nevertheless, if you carefully observe and analyze what these evil individuals do and say you can start to notice their patterns and identify sociopaths. Be patient and remain vigilant. It will take time and effort to confirm whether certain superiors or co-workers lack a conscience. Remember, even trained clinicians and experienced psychologists can be fooled.

Listed below are multiple clues that expose sociopathic traits. The more of these signs you see, the greater the likelihood that someone has no conscience and is potentially dangerous to your well-being, freedom, and happiness.

1. Actions Don't Match Words

Actions always speak louder than words. Pay attention to what people say and compare with what they do. Watch how they deal with you and others. If their talk does not match their walk, it shows lack of character and integrity. They are not trustworthy. If this happens often, then those individuals are intentionally manipulating and deceiving you—classic signs of sociopathic behavior.

2. Pathological Lying, The Rule of Threes

Sociopaths lie constantly. They habitually distort the truth. They lie without shame or remorse. They lie with impunity. They lie about important issues and insignificant things. They lie to control you. Sociopaths make promises they never intend to keep. They tell you what you want to hear, not what's true. They lie to disorient you. They lie to mess with you.

They even lie for no apparent reason. When caught lying, psychopaths concoct more lies to cover it up or rationalize it away. They have explanations for everything; some are so preposterous and unbelievable you want to burst out laughing. They continue to lie even when confronted with undeniable evidence of their lies; they look you straight in the eyes and lie: "I'm not lying."

Employ Dr. Stout's "Rule of Threes" to recognize deceivers faster. To paraphrase her advice: just one lie or one broken promise could be a misunderstanding; two lies or two broken promises could be a serious mistake; but three lies confirm that "you're dealing with a liar, and deceit is the linchpin of conscienceless behavior," warns Dr. Stout.

3. Saying Anything to Win Arguments, Gaslighting

Sociopaths say and do anything to win an argument; it doesn't matter how puny or insignificant the issue. Once psychopaths decide they must prevail in an exchange, they will never let it go until you give up. They twist reality to the breaking point to confuse you, fool you, and gain the upper hand. They gaslight you. Sociopaths exaggerate facts, misrepresent history, invent phony information, concoct fictional situations, and fabricate fake events, to ensure they're always the victors in arguments. The harder you defend your positions and challenge their assertions, the more incensed and menacing sociopaths become. They don't believe in the "let's agree to disagree" compromise. They won't let it go until you capitulate and acknowledge that they're right and you're wrong. Only then do sociopaths walk away and leave you alone. (For those unfamiliar with the term, to "gaslight" means to maliciously psychologically manipulate others by making them question their own memories and judgment to the point where they start believing they are going insane.)

4. Failure to Answer Direct Questions

"Psychopaths will not only deny the past and trivialize it, but will avoid answering your questions directly, and even if they seem to answer them—you can be sure that it's not the answer you were looking for. It has been said that even when they do give you a straight answer, the real issue will never be addressed by them," explains Dr. Robert D. Hare. Psychopaths employ several deceptive techniques. When you ask a direct question they either: (1) stay silent, (2) pretend they didn't hear your question, (3) give you an answer that has nothing to do with your question, (4) provide an answer that's ambiguous or meaningless, or (5) change the subject and act as if you never asked the question.

5. Selective and Temporary Amnesia

Sociopaths are great at "forgetting" facts, events, and information that support your points of view and contradict their lies and distortions. This selective amnesia is magically cured within hours and even seconds of its appearance. Psychopaths remember perfectly well—in great detail—any tidbit of information that favors their version of events, especially when they hold *you* accountable for your behavior or promises.

The temporary amnesia suddenly reappears when you confront sociopaths regarding other falsehoods and broken promises. Only to be immediately cured again when they recall some small mistake or minor misstatement you made. This cycle of temporary amnesia and instant cure can go on indefinitely.

6. Lack of Empathy

Sociopaths only care about themselves, they have no concern for others. They're cold-hearted. "They have no trace of empathy and no genuine interest in bonding emotionally with a mate," remarks Dr. Stout. They also don't bond emotionally with partners, friends, co-workers, or employees. Psychopaths cannot empathize with the suffering and harm they inflict on other human beings. Typically lack of empathy is evidenced by: (1) abnormal emotional responses that don't match certain situations, (2) indifference, grins, or inappropriate laughter when others are suffering, (3) crude remarks that are out of place, (4) making fun of people in pain, and (5) no remorse, shame, or regret following abusive or callous behavior.

7. Blame Game

Nothing is ever the fault of sociopaths. They will blame you for everything, even when you haven't done anything wrong. Psychopaths will victimize you and then claim you were the one responsible for the abuse they inflicted on you. Your reasonable actions or responses will be twisted around and used against you as proof of your fault; they will be misrepresented as the main reason for the sociopaths' reprimands or cruelty. Phrases like "You made me do it" or "It's all your fault" are clues that psychopaths are playing the blame game.

8. Laws of Physics Suspended, Technology Malfunctions

The laws of physics often get suspended around psychopaths. Technology frequently malfunctions near them. This must be related to the "disturbance in the Force" experiences I mentioned in the previous chapter. Emails successfully sent are never received. Recorded voicemails disappear on their own. Text messages vanish for no apparent reason. Critical files erase themselves. Computer equipment stops working, networks lose connectivity, and software applications crash without cause. All of these events have one thing in common. They always happen at the most opportune time for the sociopaths and the worst time for you. The supposed mishaps allow the psychopaths to keep lying and prevent you from challenging their falsehoods. The imaginary malfunctions help the sociopaths escape accountability, while you're rendered defenseless and left holding the bag.

9. Flattery and Charm

Psychopaths use flattery to influence and undermine you. They use intense charm to camouflage their malevolence and deceive you. Sincere compliments and genuine praise for valid reasons are fine in everyday conversations. "In contrast, flattery is extreme, and appeals to our egos in unrealistic ways. It is the material of counterfeit charm, and nearly always involves an intent to manipulate," warns Dr. Stout.

Sociopaths know they cannot constantly mistreat and humiliate you. You would eventually reach your breaking point and quit. You would escape the reach and control of the sociopath (although some find ways to manipulate you even outside the workplace). To confuse you, temporarily mitigate their abuse, and briefly make you feel better, sociopaths turn on the charm; they flatter you. They shower you with excessive praise to appeal to your ego and desire to be appreciated. It helps them maintain control. "When a sociopath identifies someone as a good game piece, she studies that person. She make it her business to know how that person can be manipulated and used, and, to this end, just how her chosen pawn can be flattered and charmed," cautions Dr. Stout.

Sometimes psychopaths offer you financial rewards and make unrealistic promises of advancement to placate you and prevent you from leaving. They frequently reference their flattery and benevolence to convince you that they're not evil and make you feel guilty for doubting them. This con game is so powerful, you start to question your own judgment and sanity. You may even feel bad about questioning the sociopaths' intentions. By disorienting you and weakening your resolve to fight back and escape, sociopaths keep you close to torment you further. They continue to play with your life. It's a diabolical, yet effective, scheme they employ. Most good and normal people have no idea what's going on—they fall for it, over and over again. I should know, I was once one of those people who got played.

10. Crocodile Tears, The Pity Play

One of the most successful, and least recognized, manipulation techniques used by sociopaths is the "pity play." Dr. Stout considers it the "best clue" for identifying those without a conscience. "The most reliable sign, the most universal behavior of unscrupulous people is not directed, as one might imagine, at our fearfulness. It is, perversely, an appeal to our sympathy," explains Dr. Stout.

In the pity play sociopaths pull out the victim card for maximum effect. They use your own conscience against you. They exploit your emotional vulnerability to manipulate you into feeling badly for them and letting your guard down. "When we pity, we are, at least for the moment, defenseless," warns Dr. Stout. Sociopaths misuse your natural sympathy towards victims to make you do what they want.

For added drama, psychopaths can act depressed or despondent. They can also turn on the waterworks on cue. "Crocodile tears at will are a sociopathic trademark," remarks Dr. Stout. Hysterical crying is also an underhanded way to shut down any rational discussions; it forces you to back down so psychopaths can get away with their schemes and win arguments. Pretending to be victims helps sociopaths hide their wickedness, while they take advantage of your kindness and decency to benefit themselves, mess with your mind, and have fun at your expense.

How to Protect Yourself

As individuals, people of conscience can learn to recognize "the sociopath next door," and with that knowledge work to defeat his entirely self-interested aims.
—Martha Stout, PhD

Once you have identified a sociopath, what should you do? Can you shield yourself from the nefarious schemes and dangerous manipulations of sociopathic bosses or co-workers? It is possible to match wits with individuals who have no conscience? Can you outsmart them?

Included below are several suggestions of how to deal with and protect yourself from sociopaths. This advice is based on some of Dr. Stout's recommendations plus my own research and insights gained in dealing with multiple sociopaths.

1. End All Contact and Keep Your Distance
If feasible, end all contact with sociopaths as soon as possible and as quickly as possible. Keeping your distance from the conscienceless is the safest way to deal with them. "The only

truly effective method for dealing with a sociopath you have identified is to disallow him or her from your life altogether," urges Dr. Stout. Break off all contact with sociopaths and place as much distance between you and them as possible. The best way to protect yourself from sociopaths is to avoid them altogether and "refuse any kind of contact or communication," recommends Dr. Stout. Don't respond and don't give in to their attempts to get in touch with you. Don't believe any of their excuses, apologies, enticements, or promises. They cannot be trusted. Warn close family and friends to also end contact with and keep their distance from those same sociopaths, if your loved ones have any dealings with them.

2. Minimize Contact, Steel Your Resolve

If you cannot break off contact with or keep your distance from sociopaths, do everything you can to minimize your interactions with them. "If total avoidance is impossible, make plans to come as close as you can to the goal of total avoidance," advises Dr. Stout. If you can't quit your job right away, prepare yourself for battle. Steel yourself mentally and spiritually to endure, resist, and fight back until you're able to leave. Use the additional guidance in this chapter to defend yourself and minimize the psychological, spiritual, and financial damage sociopath can inflict.

3. Stop Sharing Personal Information Immediately

The instant you suspect that someone's a sociopath, immediately stop sharing all personal information with that person. Everything will be used against you! Don't mention any future plans for your professional career or entrepreneurial aspirations. Don't tell them about any side business, supplementary part-time job, or additional consulting work you're doing or want to consider. Don't talk about going back to school or getting an advanced university degree. Don't say anything about your personal life, your spouse, family, or friends. Don't share anything about your hopes, dreams, or aspirations. Don't mention anything about your personal problems, fears, apprehensions, heartbreaks, or disagreements with friends, family, or your spouse. Sociopaths will use all that information against you every chance they get. They will either use it directly to bully, demoralize, and intimidate you, or indirectly to destabilize, confuse, and undermine you.

4. Silence is Your Best Friend

As much as you can, as often as you're able, remain silent. Keep your personal life as private as possible. Resist the temptation to socialize with sociopaths and anyone close to them. Don't reveal anything important about yourself or share any non-work-related opinions. Even your work commentary should be as neutral and politically correct as possible. You want to fade into the background and have the sociopath leave you alone. Becoming more reserved may reduce the sociopath's interest in you. You won't necessarily feel better (sociopaths suck the joy out of you), but you'll have more breathing space and peace of mind at work.

5. Gradually Change Your Demeanor, Don't Arouse Suspicion

If you are a happy, talkative, or gregarious person, don't suddenly become quiet and reserved. It will alert sociopaths that something is different with you. Remember, they specialize in studying and manipulating others and are quite adept at reading body language. They will notice your change in demeanor. They'll want to know "what's wrong" with you. And if your explanations don't sound genuine, you'll further raise their suspicions. So, when you tone down your style and outward behavior do it slowly and gradually to avoid detection.

If your psychopathic boss does notice and asks probing questions, make up a simple and believable excuse. Think of one beforehand and practice saying it a few times. This helps you stay calm and come across as sincere when you answer. Don't change your excuse and don't embellish it further; you risk being trapped by the experienced sociopath. Make sure it's a long-term excuse that you can deploy repeatedly to deflect suspicion for as long as possible.

6. Trust Nothing, Verify Everything

When dealing with sociopaths never trust anything they say or do. Always question their motives. Be skeptical and careful about all your interactions with them. Research and verify everything they tell you, especially if it affects your job, reputation, compensation, or future with the organization. Remember that actions speak louder than words. Closely observe the conduct and body language of sociopaths to gather important clues of their true intentions. Write things down, especially when you sense that you're being bullied, lied to, or manipulated. Keep detailed notes for yourself to have an accurate record of what's really happening and use for an objective basis of comparison. Writing things down makes it easier to spot discrepancies, obfuscations, and lies. Written notes can also help you defend yourself from, or at least briefly neutralize, the threats or abuses of workplace sociopaths.

7. Ask for Things in Writing

Start to ask for things in writing—as often as possible—especially regarding key workplace projects or significant matters related to your job. You need proper documentation to protect yourself and limit the scope and extent of the distortions sociopaths deploy. This may not necessarily work. Psychopaths are not stupid. They don't like to be held accountable. They may refuse to put anything in writing. They know that written documentation constricts their lying ability and can be used as evidence against them. They will not write things down if they can help it. However, it doesn't hurt to ask. Be as polite and professional as possible when you request it. If they ignore you or refuse, ask again. Meanwhile use the stall technique described below.

Written confirmation can also be useful if sociopathic managers promise you a future raise or promotion. Having it in writing won't guarantee that sociopaths will follow through on such promises, but at least it will prevent them from denying that they ever made those promises. It won't get you that raise or promotion, but as least you'll be spared the indignity of having to accept their denials as fact.

8. Stall or Delay

If you sense that you're being setup to fail or you suspect that your boss is trying to trap you, delay doing what he asks until he puts it in writing. Stall and keep making reasonable and believable excuses why you cannot do it until written confirmation is in hand. This may get uncomfortable. Psychopaths don't leave paper trails of their malfeasance. He'll pressure you to get it done without any written confirmation. Resist as much as you can, without getting into trouble or violating work policies. If the issue is serious enough (extremely important project, big financial risks, dangerous decision, potential legal liability, etc.), it may be worth losing your job, rather than risk ruining your reputation, damaging your career, or facing jail time. Otherwise, if you trust the sociopath's verbal reassurances and something serious does go wrong, you'll be blamed for it. Without a written record of what your sociopathic boss directed you to do and the parameters he provided, you will have no concrete proof to defend yourself with. It will be your word against his. And guess who's going to win that battle? It's definitely not going to be you.

9. Never Tell Sociopaths You Know They're Sociopaths

Never reveal to sociopaths that you know they're sociopaths. It does nothing to change their behavior and it makes things worse for you—you become a bigger target for their abuse. Sociopaths love remaining invisible. They don't like being exposed. They feel threatened by anyone who uncovers their contemptible nature. They will now intensify their efforts to control you, demoralize you, or remove you from the organization. Keep this valuable knowledge to yourself and use it to inform and guide all your decisions and actions.

10. Don't Show Weakness, Be Firm

Never signal weakness or show fear. Sociopaths thrive on sensing your fear. They feed on it. It emboldens them. It fuels their ego. It confirms how smart and cunning they are, and what a fool you are. Psychopaths see it as "winning" the game.

Don't attempt to appease sociopaths. Don't expose your vulnerability and apprehension to get them to back off. You may think you're placating them or appealing to their conscience. But they don't have a conscience. They lack empathy. Your appeals for compassion and kindness will have the opposite effect. Psychopaths will turn up the heat to watch you squirm and plead for mercy. They revel in your suffering; the more the better. Don't give them that satisfaction. Be steadfast and firm. Be polite, but maintain a serious demeanor. Don't be a pushover. Don't be rude or aggressive, but remain calm and stand your ground whenever possible. It sounds counterintuitive, but your self-assured stance will earn you more respect than being compliant and appeasing.

11. Dig Your Tunnel

You cannot waste your life fighting against and protecting yourself from sociopaths at work. Those are only shorter term tactics to use when you cannot quit your job, when you are unable to immediately leave your organization. Employ all the advice provided in earlier chapters to dig your tunnel and escape the influence and control of these toxic and shameless individuals. Do your utmost to get away from sociopaths.

Note: I followed Dr. Stout's approach and used the terms "sociopath" and "psychopath" interchangeably when referring to individuals with "antisocial personality disorder." All the guidance and suggestions I provided are based on my own experiences and extensive research on the subject of *sociopathy.* I am not a trained psychologist and I do not pretend to be one. Please take my advice with a grain of salt and conduct more in-depth research on your own. I highly recommend seeking help from a professional psychologist to address any serious or dangerous situations involving a sociopathic person that's affecting your life.

Face the Brutal Facts,
Stay Positive, Be Pragmatic

*You must never confuse faith that you will prevail in the
end—which you can never afford to lose—with the discipline
to confront the most brutal facts of your current reality,
whatever they might be.*
—James Stockdale

If you wish to regain your freedom, you must first confront
the brutal reality of your current circumstances. And for
many of you, they are harsh and awful facts. Multiple chapters in this book document the countless dysfunctions and
abuses that have become normalized across companies and
organizations. These are not isolated incidents. Historical
data has consistently shown (see Chapter 9) there is only a
30% chance that you work for a healthy organization or a
great company. This means that roughly 70% of you are employed by an average, mediocre, dysfunctional, or toxic
organization. A majority of you are either mismanaged or
mistreated by your superiors. Some of you may be abused by
a sociopathic manager or traumatized by a psychopathic boss.
That's the sobering reality you will continue to face if nothing changes, if you accept your fate, and don't take proactive
steps to defend yourself and earn back your freedom.

I wish things were different. I wish I could say something more comforting and reassuring. But I must tell you what I know to be true. Only the truth can set you free. Only the truth can help you recover your freedom and restore your joy. "If you look for truth, you may find comfort in the end: if you look for comfort you will not get either comfort or truth—only soft soap and wishful thinking to begin with and, in the end, despair," rightly proclaims C.S. Lewis. This has been the story of my own life and many others who have sought genuine freedom and happiness. I wish someone had revealed these truths to me decades ago. I wish a book like this existed in my youth. This is why I'm writing it now, to warn and help you.

The good news is that now you know. The veil of deception has been lifted. The scales have fallen from your eyes. You're seeing reality as it really is. The manipulators, abusers, and sociopaths have been exposed. They have lost their power over you. While they still control your paycheck, they no longer control your destiny. While they still influence your current financial freedom, their power to demoralize you and undermine your mental freedom has been annihilated. Now you can stop believing the lies and protect yourself from their unconscionable behavior. Now you can stop giving your pearls before swine, and start digging your tunnel to escape and seek your freedom elsewhere.

Be Alert and Remain Vigilant

What separates people, Stockdale taught me, is not the presence or absence of difficulty, but how they deal with the inevitable difficulties of life.
—Jim Collins

Remain vigilant, even if you currently work for a healthy organization and report to a great boss; even if you are enjoying your job and feel secure in your present position. Things can change in the blink of an eye. Your wonderful boss may get promoted, retire, or resign. He or she may accept a better position in a different organization and leave; a not-so-great manager may now become your new boss. Your company may be acquired by a larger corporation that makes management changes and establishes a different workplace culture. New executives may replace your current boss with someone else who doesn't like you or appreciate you as much as your previous manager. You will suddenly find yourself dreading your job and despising your new boss.

Changing economic conditions can wreck havoc on your industry and make things increasingly difficult for management; they can lead to lower pay or layoffs. You may find yourself having to start over at another organization.

Free-market economies are dynamic and change constantly. Skills and jobs that were previously sought after and in high demand can quickly become less marketable or obsolete. Entire segments of the marketplace can be disrupted and radically transformed in a matter of a few years. If you are not prepared and ready to deal with these changes, you will suffer setbacks. You will be forced to change careers whether you like it or not. This is why you need to achieve some level of financial freedom, and eventually reach mental and economic freedom.

Think Positive and Stay Positive, Realistically

A man who is self-reliant, positive, optimistic, and undertakes his work with the assurance of success magnetizes his

condition. He draws to himself the creative powers
of the universe.
—Norman Vincent Peale

Think positive and be positive to effectively pursue your freedom and happiness. A positive mental attitude is required to achieve anything meaningful in life, either professionally or personally. Good, wholesome, and constructive thoughts bring out the best in you. They allow you to move in the right direction. They boost your self-confidence. They fuel your passion, creativity, and motivation. They facilitate your change and transformation into a better version of yourself. They inspire you to take action, pursue your goals and dreams, and stay the course in the face of adversity and failure. They ultimately determine your destiny.

Frank Outlaw said it best, "Watch your thoughts, they become words; watch your words, they become actions; watch your actions, they become habits; watch your habits, they become character; watch your character, for it becomes your destiny." That is universally true for everyone. We are what we think. We become what our thoughts dictate.

The real battleground is in your heart and mind. That is where negative feelings and negative thoughts originate. That is where fears, doubts, anxieties, and apprehensions arise. If you allow them to persist and fester they will begin to dominate your mind and heart. They will overwhelm you and negatively affect your behavior, your personality, and your life. They can eventually undermine your future. Discipline your mind to focus on positive thinking and minimize negative thoughts. Train your heart to embrace positive feelings and curtail negative emotions. That doesn't mean you stop feeling bad or sad. It doesn't mean you can banish all your negative thoughts; we're human beings, not machines. But it does mean that when unreasonable negative thoughts and pessimistic feelings rear their ugly and depressive heads, you quickly take action to prevent them from taking over. Keep your emotions in check and steer our mind and heart in a positive direction.

Constant negative thoughts and negative thinking sap your creative energy, cloud your mind, undermine your self-confidence, and destroy your inspiration and motivation. Many self-help books get this right. Where some books miss the mark, is when they either preach an idealized form of optimism, confuse pragmatic realism with "negative thoughts," or imply that by identifying negative issues we somehow "attract" unfavorable outcomes. That's not true.

Don't get me wrong. I'm not saying that being an optimist is a solution to all problems. Being optimistic and positive are goals to strive toward, not a constant state of being. None of us can do it constantly or perfectly. We are human after all. But, if we want to change or achieve anything worthwhile in life, we should start from a positive frame of mind and maintain a positive attitude as often as possible to give our-selves the best chance for success.

Be a Pragmatic Optimist

Thinking positive thoughts and staying positive doesn't mean you ignore reality or disregard the dysfunctional individuals and negative things in your workplace or your life. Identify and admit the negatives, but don't dwell on them. Don't waste your energy trying to change things that you have no power to change. Be pragmatic and find realistic alternatives.

For example, if you discover that your boss is a sociopath, there's nothing you can do to help him. There is no cure for sociopathy, according to the experts. If you realize your organization is dysfunctional (most likely because the wrong people are in charge), there's little you can do to change it. One man or one woman of character cannot correct an entrenched toxic culture or a corrupt power structure. Believe me, I have tried to bring about positive and essential changes in every dysfunctional organization I have worked for and with. Each time I failed in the end. Whatever positive changes I was allowed to implement—within my sphere of influence—were eventually undone and swept away by the storm of incompetence and dysfunction that raged across the organization.

Leopards don't change their spots; sociopathic executives don't change their unconscionable behavior; and toxic organizational cultures cannot be corrected from the bottom up. The only sensible thing we can do is chart a new course for our future that minimizes, and eventually eliminates, the negative and destructive influences these workplaces have on us. That's the most practical and sensible way we can bring about meaningful change in ourselves and in our lives. That's reality, that's the truth.

Be Angry, But Do No Harm

I won't lie to you. No matter how positive you try to be, there will be days when the pain, the anger, and the resentment you experience may become too much to bear. It may happen while you read this book and realize that the injustices, indignities, and abuses you've endured at work were purposeful and calculated—used to stifle your spirit, mess with your mind, subvert your self-confidence, damage your career, or play games with your life—by an unscrupulous boss who pretended to be your mentor or friend. That kind of betrayal is hard to grasp and accept. It can crush us if we're not careful or prepared; if we don't have a solid support system behind us.

Go ahead and let the anger, resentment, and sadness wash over you. Allow yourself to mourn and come to terms with what's happened. Blow off steam by doing some intense physical activities outside or inside the house. Hit the gym or go for a vigorous walk. Call your best friend and share your misfortune. A sadness shared is half as bad, as an old Romanian saying goes. Pray or meditate. Even rage a little to express your righteous anger and indignation. Verbalize your frustration in private. Yell at the mirror, scream into your pillow, or howl at the moon. Unload your fury by writing it down in your journal, for your eyes only. It will make you feel better.

Then, take a deep breath and get busy planning your future. Start digging your tunnel. Work on regaining your freedom and restoring your joy and peace of mind. Use this book to guide and reassure you on the way.

Be angry, but do not retaliate. Don't return evil for evil. Never resort to violence. Don't do harm to anyone, human or animal (maybe swat some mosquitoes or flies, that should be ok). Channel your anger into positive energy. Let it steel your resolve. Let it fuel your determination. Reroute all your righteous indignation into positive action. Redirect your anger into planning strategies to escape the current dysfunction and toxic influence of evil individuals, and follow great personal goals.

Never return harm for the harm they have caused you. Do not stoop to their level. Success is your best revenge. Distance yourself from them and eliminate their power over you. Use the disappointment and pain as motivation for action. Direct all your physical, mental, and spiritual energy into pursuing your dreams and living a more meaningful life. Seek your true freedom and happiness; that will be your best reward. Leave the vengeance and smiting to God.

Apply and Remember

- To regain your freedom confront the brutal reality of your current circumstances.

- "If you look for truth, you may find comfort in the end: if you look for comfort you will not get either comfort or truth—only soft soap and wishful thinking to begin with and, in the end, despair." —C.S. Lewis

- Remain vigilant, even if you currently work for a healthy organization and report to a great boss; even if you are enjoying your job and feel secure in your present position. Things can change in the blink of an eye.

- A positive mental attitude is required to achieve anything meaningful in life, either professionally or personally.

- To effectively pursue your freedom and happiness strive to think positive and be positive.

- The real battleground is in your heart and your mind.

- Maintain a positive attitude as often as possible to give yourself the best chance for success.

- Be angry, but do not retaliate against who have harmed you. Don't return evil for evil.

- Channel your anger into positive energy. Let it steel your resolve. Let it fuel your determination.

- Direct all your physical, mental, and spiritual energy into pursuing your dreams and living a more meaningful life.

CHAPTER 21

Get Busy Living and Doing

The mystery of human existence lies not in just staying alive,
but in finding something to live for.

—Fyodor Dostoyevsky

Faced with the brutal reality of your current circumstances, how do you pursue your freedom and happiness? Where do you find the strength and determination to move forward? When do you start? What can you do? How do you maintain momentum?

First, be brave and make a commitment to yourself. Treat yourself as someone worth freeing and saving. Remind yourself that mere survival is not acceptable; just existing is not enough. Decide whether genuine freedom (as discussed in this book) is what you desire most. Do you really want it? If yes, then you better get busy living. Don't just think it. Don't just say it. Do it. Live your best life. Live as if you believe it. Live as if your life depended on it.

"Get busy living, or get busy dying," is the famous phrase delivered by both the "Andy Dufresne" character (played by Tim Robbins) and the Ellis Boyd "Red" Redding character (played by Morgan Freeman), in *The Shawshank Redemption* movie. The saying beautifully expresses a timeless truth: unless we make a conscious choice to live purposefully, we begin to die.

We are all going to depart this earthly life eventually; it's a tragic reality of human existence. But some people die before they die. They surrender without even trying. They accept their fate without a fight. They resign themselves to mere survival. They let their inner light go dim. They give up on their dreams. But giving up is the worst kind of death. It's abandoning hope. It's giving up on yourself. It's sentencing yourself to hopelessness. Never do that. Never surrender without a fight. Start living a purposeful and meaningful life. *Get busy living.*

Second, start doing the work. "Plans are only good intentions unless they immediately degenerate into hard work, " advises Peter F. Drucker. All your ideas, hopes, dreams, plans, and preparations don't mean much, unless you do the hard work required to turn them into reality. The sooner you take deliberate action, the better. Don't procrastinate. Don't wait until you think you're ready to begin. No one is ever really ready. If you wait for the perfect moment to arrive, you'll never start. Time is a precious and finite commodity, don't waste it just hoping, dreaming, and planning. Start today. Start now. Do the work. Take one small concrete step in the right direction. *Get busy doing.*

Practical Advice for the Journey

Once you begin living purposefully and doing the hard work, you'll need to be disciplined and tenacious to keep going and maintain your momentum. Staying positive is crucial. I already mentioned previously how a positive mindset energizes you, boosts your motivation and self-confidence, and brings out the best in you. Additionally, there are more fundamental principles that have helped me live a purposeful life and find happiness. I include below practical advice I have used to earn my freedom and become successful. Use this guidance to help you break free from dysfunctional organizations, pursue your freedom and happiness, live a meaningful life, and build long-term success.

1. Set Meaningful and Realistic Goals

Goals not only help you develop initial motivation by making your dreams obtainable, but they also help you continue to be motivated and that creates momentum.
—John C. Maxwell

To live purposefully, set specific, meaningful, and realistic goals. Goal-setting focuses your attention in the right direction. Meaningful goals energize you and motivate you to act; they positively influence your behavior. Think carefully about which goals are important to you. Write them down and create a comprehensive list. What are you passionate about? What excites you? What activities bring you joy? What work brings you personal fulfillment? What do you want to do with your life? How do you envision your future? What accomplishments will give your life meaning and purpose?

Be bold and dream big, but have both feet firmly planted in reality. Make sure your goals are clear, measurable, and achievable. Then prioritize them. Pick your top goals (for now) and make realistic and specific plans—write them down—on how to proceed and achieve those goals. Break down each goal into smaller, actionable, and more manageable steps. Honestly define and assess the corresponding tasks required for you to accomplish each step. Set concrete deadlines for each step and strive to meet them. To make the process less daunting, consider setting short-term and medium-term milestones (each supported by specific steps) that support each main goal.

Start gathering the needed resources and acquiring essential knowledge and skills. Then dedicate all your efforts and energy in pursuing those key goals. Do the tasks required to complete each step. Finish all steps needed to reach each milestone. Continually read and reference your written plans to track and evaluate your progress. Adjust your plans— milestones, steps, and tasks—to insure they remain grounded in reality and accurately reflect what you're actually doing and how you're progressing.

Select only a few goals at first to avoid being overwhelmed and distracted. Doing too many things at once will scatter your attention and diffuse your energy. It will slow you down and prevent you from reaching your most important goals. Maintain laser-like focus on just a few key goals and make incremental positive changes. Small successes, steady progress, and concrete results boost your self-confidence and motivate you to continue. They energize you. They inspire you to achieve bigger successes. Harness that energy to work harder and reach the next milestones in your plans. Once you have mastered the process, developed good habits (see below), met your original goals, and have additional freedom, energy, and time to invest in your future, you can add more goals to your list.

2. Build Good Habits, Stop Bad Habits

Depending on what they are, our habits will either make us or break us. We become what we repeatedly do.

—Sean Covey

Making plans, setting deadlines, and staying focused on your goals will not be enough. You need to develop good daily habits that support your forward progress. Your daily habits and routines will determine how effectively you implement your plans and whether you can successfully accomplish your dreams. "You'll never change your life until you change something you do daily. The secret of your success is found in your daily routine," advises John C. Maxwell.

Stop habits that waste your time, destroy your health, undermine your character, sap your energy, drain your bank account, or distract you from pursuing key goals. Better still, don't pick up bad habits to begin with. "It is easier to prevent bad habits than to break them," cautions Benjamin Franklin. If you catch yourself starting a new destructive pattern of behavior, nip it in the bud right away. You can stop quicker when the bad habit hasn't become entrenched.

If you find it difficult to establish good habits or discontinue bad habits, try a gradual approach. Attempting to change too many things at once can often backfire. People take on too much too soon, feel overwhelmed, and quit. Instead, narrow your focus and tackle just a couple of habits at a time. Downsize each habit into short and easy daily routines that require little energy and willpower to implement— sometimes called micro-habits or mini-habits. Start with small behavioral changes and slowly build up your habits until they become normal parts of your daily routine. The aim is to build consistency and become comfortable with the changes. The much smaller daily thresholds of mini-habits reduce the stress on your mind and body, and make it easier for you to practice them regularly. This in turn boosts your confidence and motivation, making it much more likely that you'll keep going and successfully establish good habits or effectively end bad habits.

For example, if your goal is to get in shape and you want a 100-pushups-per-day habit, instead of starting with 50 or 100 pushups a day, start with just 10 pushups. Stick with 10 pushups for a few days to let your body and mind adjust, then increase it to 12 pushups per day. Once you get comfortable with 12 daily pushups expand to 15, and so on. Keep slowly increasing your daily total until you reach your habit objective of 100 pushups a day.

It may take you, on average, at least two months for a new behavior to become a habit. According to a 2009 study on habit formation published in the *European Journal of Social Psychology*, "it took anywhere from 18 days to 254 days for people to form a new habit." The average time was 66 days for participants to establish a habit.

Realistically, it may take you anywhere from two to six months to successfully build a new habit. I have found that 77 to 120 days seems to be the average time it takes me to develop a good habit. It has taken me much longer—anywhere from six to nine months—to stop some bad habits. You will discover your own pace and comfort zone as you build good habits and end bad ones. Keep track of your habit days to stay motivated, maintain your momentum, and succeed.

3. Learn Continuously

*Continuous learning is the minimum requirement
for success in any field.*
—Brian Tracy

Lifelong learning is a fundamental skill of successful individuals. Constant learning is critical to your professional career and personal life. Continuous learning and self-improvement help you become an expert in your field and command a higher salary. Through continual learning entrepreneurs create, improve, and grow successful and profitable ventures. Lifelong learning has allowed me to regain my freedom and pursue my dreams—and facilitated the creation and completion of this book. Become a lifelong learner to secure and defend your financial, mental, and economic freedom.

Make reading a permanent habit. Read good books written by experienced authors who practice what they preach. Read good books on meaningful topics to acquire practical, real-world understanding and wisdom. Read good books carefully and deliberately so you can fully absorb and retain knowledge and gain useful insights. Re-read great books multiple times to remind yourself of important principles—put into practice what they say.

Make learning a permanent habit. Discover your own unique learning style; it makes it easier to understand and retain information and knowledge. Use any educational method or approach that suits you. Informal education is just as useful and valuable as a formal education. With so many resources available out there—especially online—you can find anything you need for free or at affordable prices. Online content, courses, and how-to videos on virtually any subject allow you to be in control and proceed at your own pace. These educational resources provide practical and useful information that you can apply immediately. You can practice what you learn much sooner than you could in a formal university course. This makes learning engaging and fun.

Learn by doing. Practice, practice, practice. There's no better way to understand, retain, and acquire new skills and abilities then by using and applying them. "No amount of reading or memorizing will make you successful in life. It is the understanding and application of wise thought which counts," writes Bob Proctor. You often learn better and faster by doing. Hands-on application and experimenting can provide practical training that's better than any book, video, or course.

Learn from your mistakes. Don't make the same mistake twice, or a least thrice. Learn from your successes. Learn from your failures; they teach you essential lessons. Learn from your trials and tribulations. Learn from the mistakes of others; don't repeat their mistakes. Learn from the successes of honorable and decent individuals; emulate their qualities and strategies, and pay attention to their warnings and advice. Listen carefully to those who have more experience, knowledge, and wisdom than you. Learn to keep learning and continue improving for the rest of your life.

4. Surround Yourself with Good People

You are the average of the five people
you spend the most time with.
— Jim Rohn

Seek the company and friendship of good and decent people,

both in your professional career and in your personal life. Work, partner, collaborate, and spend time with honest, hard-working, trustworthy, and honorable individuals. Seek the counsel of the wise. Trust and hire only people of character and integrity. Keep your distance from evil and corrupt people. Don't waste your time with lazy, selfish, and superficial persons. Never befriend dishonest, unethical, crooked, shameless, or abusive individuals. Never trust habitual liars. Break off all contact and get as far away as possible from sociopaths.

5. Follow the Opportunities, Bring Your Passion

Opportunity is missed by most people because
it is dressed in overalls and looks like work.
—Thomas Edison

"Follow your passion" is useful advice for many, but not for everyone. What if you haven't found your passion yet? What if your passion doesn't match your talent and ability, despite working tirelessly to improve your skills? Watch the audition phases of singing competition shows—like *American Idol*—and you'll see many contestants whose singing abilities don't match their passion and expectations. As Mike Rowe, host of Discover Channel's *Dirty Jobs* show, cautions, "just because you're passionate about something doesn't mean you won't suck at it." What if your passion doesn't help you pay the bills and make a decent living? What if following your passion will prevent you from reaching true freedom? What should you do then?

Just as important as following your passion is seizing the

right opportunities. Find ways to provide value to others and be compensated well. Consider alternative options to do great work and get paid handsomely. Look for jobs that are in high demand and pay great salaries. Find market niches that are not served competently by existing companies and start a profitable business that meets and exceeds the needs of customers.

When you follow the opportunity and become very good at what you do, there's a great chance you'll become passionate about what you do. Explore careers that offer you legitimate chances to perform meaningful work and you will "develop a genuine passion for the job you already have," advises Mike Rowe. Your passion will become aligned with the opportunity. You'll achieve financial success and freedom, and you'll also find happiness. At a minimum, pursuing the right opportunities will secure your future and finance your dreams. You'll earn the financial security and freedom needed to follow your passion.

6. Never Quit, Keep Going

Never quit. It is the easiest cop-out in the world. Set a goal and don't quit until you attain it. When you do attain it, set another goal, and don't quit until you reach it. Never quit.
—Bear Bryant

Never give up on your most important dreams. Make the necessary sacrifices to pursue those goals that give meaning and purpose to your life, that give you something to look forward to each day. Don't be discouraged if you have setbacks and experience failures along the way. Life is hard, for everyone. All of us struggle and fight to get through the many problems and hardships we experience. Everyone encounters unexpected events, sickness, misfortunes, and tribulations that frustrate us, that knock us down and stop us dead in our tracks. If you are knocked down and derailed from pursuing your goals, get back up, dust yourself off, and try again. Refocus and recommit to your plans and milestones. Continue doing the work necessary to pursue your most important goals. Never quit. Keep going.

7. Be Patient, Give it Time

All overnight success takes about ten years.
—Jeff Bezos

We live in a world that worships fast progress and glorifies instant gratification and superficiality. Additionally, rapid technological advancements, instant global communications, accelerating innovations, and pervasive mobile applications give the illusion that everything happens at light speed. However, significant improvements, true progress, and enduring success—for people and organizations—never happen fast. Nothing meaningful in life happens quickly. Real and lasting success takes *years* to build. If you want to accomplish anything worthwhile you have to be patient, disciplined, and persistent. It takes time and consistent effort to be successful and achieve important goals.

Don't trust anyone who offers quick results with minimal effort, especially in regards to financial investments or business ventures. "Get-rich-quick" schemes are just that, *schemes*. They promote the myth that wealth can be created easily in a short period of time. They don't work and they never bring you long-term success. Their only purpose is to enrich those who peddle those mythical schemes, not you.

As a matter of fact, achieving success—especially financial success—too easily and quickly can be a recipe for disaster. Many famous child actors, professional athletes, and lottery winners who come into their fortunes rapidly, wind up bankrupt and destitute. Some lottery winners refer to their large financial windfalls as curses rather than blessings. The millions they won ultimately ruined their relationships, shattered their marriages, and destroyed their lives, because they were not ready or prepared to handle it.

To achieve extraordinary results and become successful, you need to be focused, patient, and resolute. Invest the required energy and effort over time. Do the work. There are no shortcuts to financial and economic freedom. This is how successful individuals have done it. This is how you can achieve it. "When you see someone who has a lot of knowledge, they learned it over time. When you see someone who has a lot of skills, they developed them over time. When you see someone who has done a lot, they accomplished it over time. When you see someone who has a lot of money, they earned it over time. The key is over time. Success is built sequentially. It's one thing at a time," observes Gary Keller, the founder of Keller Williams, one of the biggest real estate franchises in the world.

Gradual, determined, and consistent positive action works wonders. Every step in the right direction brings you closer to your goals and freedom. Every smart decision, wise choice, and meaningful accomplishment in furtherance of your goals and dreams, brings you closer to happiness. Steady and incremental forward progress wins the race, every single time.

Get busy living. Get busy doing.

CHAPTER 22

Fight for Your Freedom
and Find Happiness

*Freedom is never more than one generation away from
extinction. We didn't pass it to our children in the
bloodstream. It must be fought for, protected,
and handed on for them to do the same.*

—Ronald Reagan

Freedom must be fought for and fiercely protected, always.
Freedom requires vigilance. Freedom necessitates hard work
and long-term planning. Freedom demands sacrifices. This is
true for all individuals and societies throughout history. Our
age is no different.

Unfortunately, many corporations and organizations, especially academia, governments, and politicians, do their
damndest to take freedom away from you. They despise your
independence. They're threatened when you have too much
freedom. Their unquenchable thirst for power drives them to
control your life, your property, and your liberty. They seek
to make you fully dependent on them. They want you to be
subservient to them. They get to choose, you don't. This is
not liberty, it's tyranny. It's not free-market capitalism, it's
modern feudalism.

If you want to be free you must fight for it. No one is going to hand your freedom to you. No one will give you the financial freedom, mental freedom, or economic freedom you need to be truly free. Work to earn those freedoms. Fight to gain your independence, follow your own path, and seek long-term success (as you choose to define it). Then be prepared to vigorously defend your hard-earned freedom and independence. This is a lifelong battle. It's a worthy and honorable endeavor. Fight, and you will find purpose and happiness. Surrender, and you can lose your dignity and face hopelessness and despair. The choice is yours. Choose wisely!

Find Happiness, Find Joy

If you want to be happy, set a goal that commands your thoughts, liberates your energy, and inspires your hopes.
—Andrew Carnegie

Happiness should not be your main goal. If you desire happiness for its own sake you may not necessarily find it. Instead, "seek purpose and happiness will follow as a shadow comes with the sunshine," advises William Scolavino. True happiness is typically the byproduct of you doing something meaningful. Find a noble purpose for your life. Pursue worthy goals, and be ready to sacrifice and work hard to achieve them, and you will create the right conditions for genuine happiness to appear in your life.

Remember that the happiness I hope you'll find is more accurately described as joy. It's a state of gladness and cheerfulness that is combined with peace, optimism, and contentment. Joy strengthens your mind, builds up your soul, and soothes your heart. Joy brings with it a pure goodness that illumines your heart and mind. Joy transforms you in a beneficial way and leads to your well-being and fulfillment. Even when it subsides, joy's positive and uplifting effects remain imprinted on your soul.

Bear in mind that joy is often discovered in the journey. You can find joy in your struggle for freedom. Breaking free from a dysfunctional organization is a worthy cause. Escaping the destructive and wicked manipulations of a sociopathic boss is a noble endeavor. Pursuing your freedom is meaningful. These actions bring you joy, they give you hope. Start fighting to be free and you will experience joy, even before you've found your purpose and achieved your goals.

Have Hope

Men can live for forty days without food, for four days without water, and for about four minutes without air. But they cannot live for four seconds without hope.

Human beings cannot live without hope. Hope is the fuel that powers our souls, inspires our minds, invigorates our hearts, and motivates us to act. Hope carries us through the toughest moments. Hope give us the energy to fight and do something useful with our lives. Hope helps us live life and live it more abundantly.

We all need to have a purpose in life to give meaning to our existence. Without a purpose-driven life, we waste away; we become unhappy or despondent; we give up. To paraphrase Viktor Frankl, who himself referenced Friedrich Nietzsche, those who know the "why" of their existence, will be able to bear almost any "how." Discover your "why" and you will find your hope, find your purpose, and your joy. No matter what has happened to you in the past. No matter how bad things are now at work. No matter what is going on with your life. No matter how old you are. No matter how many times adversity has knocked you down. No matter how many times you have failed before. Never lose hope. Have faith that you can overcome your tribulations and change your current situation. Never give up. Never give in to despondency or despair. Have hope and take action.

Have faith in yourself and your ability to persevere. Never give up your quest to regain your freedom and find happiness. You were created to be free. Prepare for the journey ahead and look for opportunities to do something useful, valuable, or honorable with your life. Hold on to hope and take the next step toward your destiny.

CHAPTER 23

Join the Revolution, Help Others

If you have an opportunity to help others or incite change,
it feels like a moral obligation to do so.

—Elizabeth Chambers

I hope this book has helped you in all the ways I intended. I hope it has opened your eyes to universal principles and wisdom that you can use in your own life. I hope it has comforted and reassured you. I hope it has convinced you to dig your tunnel, break free from dysfunctional organizations, and escape the influence of toxic individuals. I hope it has motivated you to pursue true freedom and happiness. I hope it has given you hope. I hope it has inspired you to live a meaningful life.

If you liked this book and believe in its purpose, message, and mission; and you desire to help and free others; and you want to join this peaceful and creative revolution, there are several ways you can support this worthy endeavor:

1. Write a Book Review, Share Your Story

Write a book review. Describe how the book has helped you specifically. Highlight which recommendations were most practical or useful. Share your story with others so they will be inspired by your experiences and insights. Your hope and courage can motivate others who currently face similar circumstances. Your pursuit of freedom can encourage others to begin their journeys. Your joy will illuminate the path for others to follow in your footsteps.

2. Recommend the Book to Others

Help free others. If you know others who can benefit from this book, please recommend it. Let them know how this book has positively influenced your life and why you think they should read it also. Share with them a few examples from the book so they understand the unique character and purpose of the content.

3. Gift a Book to Friends and Family

Surprise close friends and family members by giving them a copy of this book as a gift. Help them change their lives for the better and taste real freedom. It's always nicer to give than to receive. Better still, the book can be a gift that keeps on giving if it inspires and motivates them to pursue their freedom and happiness.

4. Give a Book to Someone in Need

If you're aware of someone struggling financially and professionally who could genuinely use the guidance this book provides, buy a copy and give it to him or her. There is great joy in giving. There is added joy when you're giving someone else a chance to find freedom and experience true happiness.

Thank You

Thank you for taking this journey with me. Thank you for trusting me with your time. I welcome you to visit www.ChrisBanescu.com for additional practical advice, inspiration, and motivation to continue to pursue and preserve your freedom and happiness.

Acknowledgments

First and foremost I would like to thank God for the life He has given me and the many blessings He has bestowed upon me. Thank you Lord for the wellspring of inspiration and wisdom You have provided to help me complete this book.

I am grateful for my wife Cindy and my daughter Elizabeth. Your patience, love, and support helped me bring this project to completion. Cindy, you were especially charitable in listening to me read out loud multiple versions of each chapter. Elizabeth, your proofreading skills improved many sections. Both of you have made this book better.

I lift up to heaven a special thank you to my grandfather, Father Basil, who took on the role of my own father from the time I was six. Your example, unconditional love, guidance, prayers, and constant nurturing of my Orthodox Christian faith helped me mature, acquire wisdom, and discover my true vocation in life.

A heartfelt thank you goes to my best and dearest friend Magdy Baiady. Your love, kindness, and experienced counsel have been spiritual oxygen to my heart and soul. Our close friendship has brought great joy into my life. Your positive reaction and your family's supportive comments upon hearing a few early chapters confirmed that I was moving in the right direction.

Another thank you goes to Father Johannes Jacobse, my good friend and fellow truth warrior. I am grateful for your prayers, wisdom, and reassurances that gave me hope, and motivated me to follow my calling and complete this book.

Finally, I would like to thank my students. For more than two decades your enthusiastic support and encouraging feedback continually reminded me that something special was happening in our courses—something that needed to be shared with others. Your gracious comments and life experiences sparked the idea for this book. I am forever grateful for your kindness and support.

About the Author

Chris Banescu, JD, an entrepreneur, small business owner, and university professor, is a leadership and management expert with a passion for excellence and common sense. His career experience spans small and medium-sized companies, large corporations, traditional and online universities, and several e-commerce entrepreneurial ventures. He has taught a variety of business, law, ethics, finance, entrepreneurship, information technology, leadership, management, and e-commerce courses at the graduate and undergraduate level for multiple universities—including Woodbury University, the University of Maryland Global Campus, and Capella University. He holds a Bachelor of Science degree from New York University and a Juris Doctor degree from Southwestern University School of Law.

Visit Chris Banescu on the web at
www.ChrisBanescu.com.

Made in the USA
Coppell, TX
26 September 2020